MW00952998

Keto Air Fryer Cookbook for Beginners

1000+ Days of Amazing, Low Carb and High-fat Recipes.

Ketogenic Diet for Effective and Healthy Lifestyle

EVA HARMON

Disclaimer

The information contained in this cookbook is intended for general knowledge and informational purposes only, and does not constitute medical advice. The author is not a medical professional, and the recipes and information provided are not intended to diagnose, treat, cure, or prevent any disease or health condition. Before making any changes to your diet or lifestyle, it is essential to consult with a qualified healthcare professional.

The author assumes no responsibility for any injury, illness, or other adverse effects that may result from the use or misuse of the information contained in this cookbook.

The recipes in this cookbook are intended as a starting point and may need to be adjusted to suit individual dietary needs and preferences.

It is recommended to use caution when preparing and consuming any food, and to always follow safe food handling practices.

This cookbook may contain affiliate links. This means that if you click on a link and make a purchase, the author may receive a small commission at no extra cost to you.

Copyright © 2024 EVA HARMON

All rights reserved. No part of this publication may be reproduced, distributed, or transmitted in any form or by any means, including photocopying, recording, or other electronic or mechanical methods, without the prior written permission of the author, except in the case of brief quotations embodied in critical reviews and certain other noncommercial uses permitted by copyright law.

Table of Contents

Introduction

• What is the Keto Diet?

The Ketogenic diet, or simply Keto, is more than just a fad. It's a way of eating that has been around for decades, gaining renewed popularity for its potential health benefits and effectiveness in managing weight. Unlike traditional diets that emphasize carbohydrates, the Keto diet focuses on maximizing fat intake while drastically reducing carbohydrates. This shift in fuel source forces your body to enter a metabolic state called ketosis, where it starts burning fat for energy instead of glucose (sugar).

• Understanding the Keto Foundation

The core principle of the Keto diet lies in its macronutrient breakdown:

- **High Fat:** 70-80% of your daily calories should come from healthy fats like avocado, olive oil, nuts, and fat fish.
- **Moderate Protein:** 15-20% of your daily calories should be from protein sources like lean meats, eggs, and dairy.
- **Low Carbohydrates:** 5-10% of your daily calories come from low-carb vegetables like leafy greens, broccoli, and cauliflower.

• Health Benefits of the Keto Diet

Beyond weight loss, the Keto diet has been linked to a range of health benefits:

- **Improved Blood Sugar Control:** By limiting carbohydrates, the Keto diet can help regulate blood sugar levels, which is particularly beneficial for individuals with type 2 diabetes.
- **Enhanced Brain Function:** The brain thrives on ketones, the by-product of fat metabolism. The Keto diet may improve cognitive function, focus, and memory.
- **Reduced Inflammation:** Inflammation is linked to numerous chronic diseases. The anti-inflammatory properties of the Keto diet can contribute to overall health.
- **Increased Energy Levels:** Many people report experiencing increased energy and a reduced feeling of "fogginess" after adopting a Keto lifestyle.

• The Keto-Approved Foods

1. Healthy Fats:
- **Avocado:** This creamy fruit is brimming with monounsaturated fats, fiber, and essential vitamins and minerals. Enjoy it as a snack, in salads, or as a base for guacamole.
- **Olive Oil:** A powerhouse of monounsaturated fats, olive oil is a versatile cooking oil and a key ingredient in dressings and marinades. Opt for extra virgin olive oil for maximum flavor and health benefits.
- **Nuts and Seeds:** Almonds, walnuts, chia seeds, and flaxseeds are excellent sources of healthy fats, protein, and fiber. Enjoy them as snacks or incorporate them into smoothies and meals.
- **Full-Fat Dairy:** Choose full-fat yogurt, cheese, and cream for their healthy fats and protein content. Look for organic, grass-fed options for optimal nutritional value.
- **Fatty Fish:** Salmon, mackerel, tuna, and sardines are rich in omega-3 fatty acids, essential for brain health and reducing inflammation. Enjoy them grilled, baked, or poached.
- **Eggs:** Eggs are a versatile source of protein and healthy fats. Experiment with different cooking methods to enjoy their delicious flavor and nutritional benefits.

2. Protein:
- **Meat:** Lean meats like chicken, turkey and beef provide essential protein and nutrients. Choose grass-fed and organic options whenever possible.

- **Seafood:** Enjoy a variety of fish for their protein and healthy fats. Explore different cooking methods to add variety to your meals.
- **Poultry:** Chicken and turkey offer lean protein and can be incorporated into various dishes, from soups to stir-fries.
- **Tofu and Tempeh:** For vegetarians and vegans, tofu and tempeh provide plant-based protein sources that can be used in countless recipes.

3. Low-Carb Vegetables:
- **Leafy Greens:** Spinach, kale, romaine lettuce, and other leafy greens are low in carbs and rich in vitamins, minerals, and antioxidants. Enjoy them raw in salads, sautéed in olive oil, or blended into smoothies.
- **Cruciferous Vegetables:** Broccoli, cauliflower, Brussels sprouts, and cabbage are excellent sources of fiber and nutrients. Experiment with different cooking methods, from steaming to roasting, to enhance their flavor.
- **Other Low-Carb Vegetables:** Zucchini, asparagus, mushrooms, bell peppers, and onions are versatile and flavorful options that fit perfectly into a Keto diet.

Foods to Avoid or Limit on the Keto Diet

The Keto diet requires significant restrictions on carbohydrate intake, which means certain foods need to be avoided or limited:
- **Sugary Foods:** This includes processed foods, desserts, candy, sodas, fruit juices, and any foods with added sugar.
- **Starchy Vegetables:** Potatoes, corn, peas, and other starchy vegetables are high in carbohydrates and should be limited or avoided altogether.
- **Grains:** Bread, pasta, rice, cereal, and other grain-based products are high in carbohydrates and should be eliminated on a strict Keto diet.
- **Legumes:** Beans, lentils, and chickpeas are high in carbohydrates and can negatively impact ketosis.
- **Fruits:** While some fruits like berries are lower in carbohydrates, most fruits should be avoided or limited on the Keto diet.
- **Alcohol:** Alcoholic beverages are high in carbohydrates and can interfere with ketosis.
- **Artificial Sweeteners:** While some artificial sweeteners are low in carbohydrates, they can disrupt gut health and have other potential adverse effects.

Tips for Beginners

Making the transition to Keto doesn't have to be overwhelming. Start with small changes:
- **Simple Swaps:** Swap out sugary drinks for water, unsweetened tea, or sparkling water. Replace pasta and rice with cauliflower rice.
- **Meal Planning:** Plan your meals ahead of time to avoid impulsive choices. Prepare large batches of Keto-friendly dishes for easy meals throughout the week.
- **Smart Shopping:** Stock your pantry with healthy fats like avocado oil, coconut oil, and nuts. Opt for fresh vegetables and lean protein sources.
- **Embrace Keto Cuisine:** Experiment with delicious Keto recipes that include healthy fats, protein, and low-carb vegetables.
- **Focus on Healthy Fats and Protein:** Prioritize meals that are rich in healthy fats and protein to keep you feeling satisfied and minimize cravings.
- **Prepare Snacks:** Keep healthy Keto-friendly snacks on hand to help you avoid unhealthy cravings when you're on the go.
- **Seek Support:** Connect with others on a Keto diet or join online communities to share tips, recipes, and encouragement.
- **Be Patient:** Allow yourself time to adjust to the dietary changes and embrace the process.

Embrace the Keto lifestyle and unlock your potential for a healthier, happier you!

II. <u>Air Fryer Fundamentals</u>

• Air Fryer Basics:

At its core, the air fryer is a countertop appliance designed to mimic the results of deep-frying using a fraction of the oil. It achieves this by utilizing a combination of powerful fans and heating elements to circulate hot air around food, creating a crispy exterior and a tender interior.

Unpacking the Components: Let's delve into the key components that make the air fryer tick:

- **Heating Element:** This element, typically located at the bottom of the fryer, generates heat and creates a convection current within the appliance.
- **Fan:** The fan, strategically positioned near the heating element, rapidly circulates the hot air around the food, ensuring even cooking.
- **Basket:** The removable basket holds the food and allows for air circulation and optimal cooking.
- **Timer and Temperature Controls:** These user-friendly features allow you to set the desired cooking time and temperature, ensuring consistent results.

Mastering the Settings and Features: Modern air fryers come equipped with an array of settings and features to cater to diverse culinary needs.

- **Pre-Set Programs:** Many air fryers offer pre-programmed settings for popular dishes like fries, chicken, and vegetables. These settings optimize temperature and time for best results, making cooking a breeze.
- **Temperature Control:** Allows you to adjust the temperature based on the type of food being cooked. Higher temperatures are ideal for crispy exteriors, while lower temperatures are perfect for delicate items.
- **Timer:** Enables you to set the cooking duration according to the recipe's instructions.
- **Shake Reminder:** Some air fryers have a "shake" reminder feature that prompts you to gently shake the basket mid-cooking to ensure even browning.

• Troubleshooting and Solutions:

Despite its simplicity, air fryers can encounter some common issues. Here's how to tackle them:

- **Unevenly Cooked Food:** Ensure the food is spread evenly in the basket and shake it halfway through cooking.
- **Overcooked Food:** Check the timer and adjust it accordingly, or lower the temperature.
- **Undercooked Food:** Increase the cooking time or temperature, or pre-heat the air fryer for a few minutes.
- **Burnt Food:** Reduce the cooking time or temperature, or use a lower setting for foods that easily burn.

• Maintaining and Cleaning for Longevity:
- **Regular Cleaning:** Regularly wipe the interior and exterior with a damp cloth and mild detergent.
- **Basket Care:** Wash the basket and removable parts in the dishwasher or by hand with soap and water.
- **Storage:** Store the air fryer in a cool, dry place when not in use.

A Culinary Game Changer: The air fryer, with its simple yet powerful technology, has revolutionized cooking. From crispy snacks to succulent meats, the possibilities are endless. Its efficiency, health benefits, and user-friendliness make it a valuable addition to any kitchen. By understanding the workings of this innovative appliance, you can unlock its full potential and elevate your culinary adventures to new heights.

II. Keto Air Fryer Recipes

Breakfast:

1.1 Fluffy Keto Pancakes in Minutes
Yield: 2 servings **Prep Time:** 5 minutes **Cook Time:** 5-7 minutes

Ingredients:

- 2 large eggs
- 1/4 cup unsweetened almond milk (or your preferred keto-friendly milk)
- 1 tablespoon melted coconut oil
- 1/4 cup almond flour
- 1 tablespoon psyllium husk powder
- 1 teaspoon baking powder
- 1/4 teaspoon salt

- 2 tablespoons olive oil
- 1 teaspoon garlic powder
- 1/2 teaspoon onion powder
- 1/4 teaspoon black pepper
- 1/4 teaspoon salt
- 1/4 cup chopped fresh cilantro (optional)

Instructions:

1. **Mix:** In a large bowl, whisk together eggs, almond milk, melted coconut oil, almond flour, psyllium husk powder, baking powder, salt, and vanilla extract (if using).
2. **Sweeten:** Stir in your chosen sweetener. The amount will depend on your taste preference.
3. **Prepare Air Fryer:** Preheat your air fryer to 350°F (175°C). Lightly grease the air fryer basket with butter or coconut oil.
4. **Pour Batter:** Pour batter into the prepared air fryer basket in two separate mounds, leaving some space between them.
5. **Cook:** Air fry for 5-7 minutes, or until golden brown and cooked through. You may need to shake the basket halfway through cooking for even browning.
6. **Serve:** Remove the pancakes from the air fryer and top with your favorite keto-friendly toppings. Enjoy!

Nutritional Information (per serving): Calories: 350, Protein: 18g, Carbohydrates: 7g (Net carbs: 3g), Fats: 25g, Fiber: 4g, Cholesterol: 150mg, Sodium: 200mg, Potassium: 250mg

2.1 Savory Keto Breakfast Hash
Yield: 2 servings **Prep Time:** 5 minutes **Cook Time:** 10-12 minutes

Ingredients:

- 1 pound ground beef (or ground sausage, turkey, or chicken)
- 1/2 cup chopped onion
- 1/2 cup chopped bell pepper (any color)
- 1/4 cup chopped celery
- 1/4 cup chopped mushrooms

- 2 tablespoons olive oil
- 1 teaspoon garlic powder
- 1/2 teaspoon onion powder
- 1/4 teaspoon black pepper
- 1/4 teaspoon salt
- 1/4 cup chopped fresh cilantro (optional)

Instructions:

1. **Prep the ingredients:** Chop all vegetables into bite-sized pieces.
2. **Brown the meat:** In a large bowl, combine the ground meat, onion, bell pepper, celery, mushrooms, olive oil, garlic powder, onion powder, salt, and pepper.
3. **Air fry the hash:** Transfer the meat mixture to the air fryer basket. Cook at 375°F (190°C) for 10-12 minutes, stirring every 3-4 minutes to ensure even cooking and browning.
4. **Add cilantro:** Stir in the chopped cilantro (optional) during the last minute of cooking.
5. **Serve hot:** Enjoy your savory keto breakfast hash hot, with a side of avocado or a dollop of sour cream.

Nutritional Information (per serving): Calories: 400, Protein: 30g, Carbohydrates: 5g, Fats: 25g, Fiber: 3g, Cholesterol: 100mg, Sodium: 400mg, Potassium: 500mg,

3.1 Creamy Keto Avocado Toast

Yield: 1 serving **Prep Time:** 5 minutes **Cook Time:** 7 minutes

Ingredients:

- 1 slice of keto bread (e.g., almond flour bread, coconut flour bread)
- 1/2 ripe avocado, mashed
- 1 tablespoon sour cream (or Greek yogurt)
- 1/4 teaspoon salt
- 1/4 teaspoon black pepper
- 1/4 teaspoon garlic powder (optional)
- 1/4 teaspoon paprika (optional)
- 1 tablespoon chopped fresh cilantro (optional)
- 1/2 tablespoon olive oil spray, for greasing the air fryer basket

Instructions:

1. **Prepare the avocado mixture:** Mash the avocado in a bowl. Add sour cream, salt, pepper, garlic powder (optional), and paprika (optional). Stir until well combined.
2. **Prepare the bread:** Lightly spray the air fryer basket with olive oil spray. Place the slice of keto bread in th basket.
3. **Air fry the bread:** Cook the bread at 350°F (175°C) for 3-5 minutes, or until lightly toasted and crisp.
4. **Assemble the toast:** Spread the avocado mixture evenly over the toasted bread.
5. **Add cilantro:** Sprinkle with chopped cilantro (optional) for added freshness.

Nutritional Information (per serving): Calories: 350, Protein: 10g, Carbohydrates: 10g, Fats: 25g, Fiber: 5g, Cholesterol: 30mg, Sodium: 200mg, Potassium: 600mg

4.1 Air Fryer Keto Cinnamon Rolls

Yield: 4 servings **Prep Time:** 10 minutes **Cook Time:** 8-10 minutes

Ingredients:
Dough:

- 1 cup almond flour
- 1/4 cup coconut flour
- 1 teaspoon baking powder
- 1/4 teaspoon salt
- 1/4 cup melted butter
- 1/4 cup unsweetened almond milk
- 1 large egg
- 1/4 teaspoon vanilla extract

- **Filling:**
  - 1/4 cup melted butter
  - 1/4 cup erythritol or other keto-friendly sweetener
  - 2 tablespoons cinnamon
  - 1/4 teaspoon ground nutmeg (optional)

- **Frosting:**
  - 4 tablespoons softened cream cheese
  - 1 tablespoon unsalted butter, softened
  - 1/4 cup erythritol or other keto-friendly sweetener
  - 1 teaspoon vanilla extract
  - 1 tablespoon heavy cream (optional)

Instructions:

1. **Prepare the dough:** In a large bowl, whisk together the almond flour, coconut flour, baking powder, and sa
2. **Combine wet ingredients:** In a separate bowl, whisk together the melted butter, almond milk, egg, and vanilla extract.
3. **Mix dough:** Gradually add the wet ingredients to the dry ingredients, mixing until a soft dough forms.
4. **Prepare the filling:** In a small bowl, combine the melted butter, sweetener, cinnamon, and nutmeg (optional).
5. **Assemble the rolls:** Divide the dough into 4 equal portions. Roll each portion into a rectangle about 6 inch long and 3 inches wide. Spread the cinnamon filling evenly over each rectangle.
6. **Roll the dough:** Roll up each rectangle tightly, starting from the long side.
7. **Slice the rolls:** Cut each roll into 1-inch slices.

8. **Air fry the rolls:** Lightly spray the air fryer basket with cooking spray. Arrange the cinnamon roll slices in the basket, leaving a little space between each one. Air fry at 350°F (175°C) for 8-10 minutes, or until golden brown and cooked through.
9. **Prepare the frosting:** In a small bowl, beat together the cream cheese, butter, sweetener, vanilla extract, and heavy cream (optional) until smooth.
10. **Frost the rolls:** Once the rolls are cooked, spread a generous amount of frosting over each one. Serve warm and enjoy! For added texture, sprinkle chopped pecans or walnuts on top of the frosting.

Nutritional Information (per serving): Calories: 350, Protein: 10g, Carbohydrates: 15g, Fats: 25g, Fiber: 5g, Cholesterol: 80mg, Sodium: 200mg, Potassium: 250mg

5.1 Sweet & Spicy Keto Breakfast Sausage
Yield: 4 servings **Prep Time:** 5 minutes **Cook Time:** 8-10 minutes

Ingredients:

- 1 pound ground beef
- 1/4 cup finely chopped onion
- 1 tablespoon maple syrup (or keto-friendly sweetener)
- 1 teaspoon smoked paprika
- 1/2 teaspoon chili powder
- 1/4 teaspoon cayenne pepper (optional, for extra spice)
- 1/4 teaspoon salt
- 1/4 teaspoon black pepper

Instructions:

1. **Combine ingredients:** In a large bowl, combine the ground beef, onion, maple syrup, smoked paprika, chili powder, cayenne pepper (optional), salt, and black pepper. Mix well until evenly distributed.
2. **Form patties:** Shape the mixture into 4-6 patties, about 1/2 inch thick.
3. **Air fry the sausage:** Preheat your air fryer to 400°F (200°C). Place the sausage patties in the air fryer basket, leaving a little space between each one.
4. **Cook:** Air fry for 8-10 minutes, flipping the patties halfway through cooking to ensure even browning.
5. **Serve immediately:** Enjoy the sweet and spicy sausage hot, with your favorite keto-friendly sides like eggs, avocado, or spinach.

Nutritional Information (per serving): Calories: 250, Protein: 20g, Carbohydrates: 2g, Fats: 16g, Fiber: 1g, Cholesterol: 70mg, Sodium: 250mg, Potassium: 200mg

6.1 Perfect Keto Omelet in a Flash
Yield: 1 serving **Prep Time:** 5 minutes **Cook Time:** 5-7 minutes

- **Ingredients:**
- 2 large eggs
- 1 tablespoon heavy cream
- 1/4 teaspoon salt
- 1/4 teaspoon black pepper
- 1 tablespoon shredded cheddar cheese (or your favorite keto-friendly cheese)
- 1/4 cup chopped spinach (optional)
- 1/4 cup diced bell pepper (optional)
- 1/4 teaspoon garlic powder (optional)
- 1/4 teaspoon onion powder (optional)
- 1 teaspoon olive oil spray, for greasing the air fryer basket

Instructions:

1. **Prepare the omelet mixture:** In a small bowl, whisk together the eggs, heavy cream, salt, and pepper.
2. **Add your favorite fillings:** Stir in the shredded cheese, spinach, bell pepper, garlic powder, and onion powder (optional).
3. **Grease the air fryer basket:** Lightly spray the air fryer basket with olive oil spray.
4. **Pour the mixture:** Pour the egg mixture into the prepared basket.
5. **Air fry the omelet:** Cook at 350°F (175°C) for 5-7 minutes, or until the omelet is set and golden brown.
6. **Check for doneness:** Use a spatula to gently lift the omelet. If it is set and easily slides out of the basket, it is done.

7. **Serve immediately:** Enjoy your perfectly cooked keto omelet hot, with a side of avocado, keto-friendly sausage, or a sprinkle of your favorite spices.

Nutritional Information (per serving): Calories: 200, Protein: 15g, Carbohydrates: 2g, Fats: 12g, Fiber: 1g, Cholesterol: 150mg, Sodium: 150mg, Potassium: 250mg

7.1 Easy Keto Egg Bites for Meal Prep
Yield: 6 servings Prep Time: 10 minutes Cook Time: 15-20 minutes

Ingredients:
- 6 large eggs
- 1/4 cup heavy cream
- 1/4 cup shredded cheddar cheese
- 1/4 cup chopped mushrooms, sautéed (optional)
- 1/4 teaspoon salt
- 1/8 teaspoon black pepper
- Pinch of garlic powder (optional)
- Pinch of onion powder (optional)
- 1 tablespoon butter, melted (for greasing)

Instructions:
1. **Prepare the egg mixture:** In a medium bowl, whisk together the eggs, heavy cream, salt, pepper, and optional spices.
2. **Add cheese and mushrooms:** Stir in the shredded cheese and sautéed mushrooms (if using).
3. **Grease the air fryer basket:** Brush the basket of your air fryer with melted butter.
4. **Pour the mixture into ramekins:** Divide the egg mixture evenly among 6 individual ramekins or silicone muffin cups.
5. **Air fry:** Place the ramekins in the air fryer basket and cook at 325°F (165°C) for 15-20 minutes, or until the egg bites are set and no longer jiggle in the center. You may need to shake the basket halfway through cooking to ensure even cooking.
6. **Rest and serve:** Let the egg bites cool slightly before serving. They can be enjoyed warm or cold.

Nutritional Information (Per Serving): Calories: 160, Protein: 12g, Carbohydrates: 2g, Fats: 13g, Fiber: 0g, Cholesterol: 250mg, Sodium: 220mg, Potassium: 100mg

8.1 Cheesy Keto Breakfast Burrito
Yield: 2 servings Prep Time: 10 minutes Cook Time: 15-20 minutes

Ingredients:
- 2 large eggs
- 1/4 cup heavy cream
- 1/4 cup shredded cheddar cheese
- 1/4 cup chopped bell peppers (any color), sautéed (optional)
- 1/4 cup chopped onions, sautéed (optional)
- 1/4 cup cooked and crumbled sausage (optional)
- 1/4 teaspoon salt
- 1/8 teaspoon black pepper
- 1 tablespoon butter, melted (for greasing)
- 2 large lettuce leaves (for burrito wraps)

Instructions:
1. **Prepare the egg mixture:** In a bowl, whisk together the eggs, heavy cream, salt, and pepper.
2. **Add cheese and fillings:** Stir in the shredded cheese, sautéed bell peppers and onions (if using), and cooked sausage (if using).
3. **Grease the air fryer basket:** Brush the basket of your air fryer with melted butter.
4. **Assemble the burritos:** Divide the egg mixture evenly onto two large lettuce leaves, spreading it out to cover the leaves almost entirely. Fold the sides of the lettuce leaves inwards and roll them up tightly.
5. **Air fry:** Place the rolled burritos in the air fryer basket and cook at 375°F (190°C) for 15-20 minutes, or until the burritos are golden brown and the egg mixture is set. You may need to flip the burritos halfway through cooking to ensure even browning.
6. **Rest and serve:** Let the burritos cool slightly before serving.

Nutritional Information (Per Serving): Calories: 300, Protein: 20g, Carbohydrates: 5g, Fats: 20g, Fiber: 2g, Cholesterol: 250mg, Sodium: 300mg, Potassium: 250mg

9.1 Keto Smoothie Bowl with Berries & Nuts

Yield: 1 serving **Prep Time:** 10 minutes **Cook Time:** 5-7 minutes (for toppings)

Ingredients:

For the Smoothie Base:

- 1 cup unsweetened almond milk
- 1/2 cup unsweetened coconut milk
- 1/4 cup unsweetened almond butter
- 1 scoop vanilla protein powder
- 1 tablespoon chia seeds
- 1 teaspoon vanilla extract
- Pinch of salt
- Optional: 1-2 tablespoons MCT oil (for extra fat and energy)

For the Air-Fried Toppings:

- 1/2 cup mixed berries (strawberries, raspberries, blueberries)
- 1/4 cup chopped walnuts or pecans
- 1 tablespoon coconut oil

Instructions:

1. **Prepare the smoothie base:** In a blender, combine all the smoothie base ingredients until smooth and creamy.
2. **Prepare the air fryer:** Preheat your air fryer to 350°F (175°C).
3. **Air fry the berries:** Toss the berries with 1 tablespoon of coconut oil. Spread them in a single layer in the air fryer basket. Cook for 5-7 minutes, shaking the basket halfway through, until the berries are slightly softened and lightly browned.
4. **Air fry the nuts:** Spread the chopped walnuts or pecans in the air fryer basket and cook for 3-5 minutes, shaking the basket occasionally, until the nuts are fragrant and lightly toasted.
5. **Assemble the bowl:** Pour the smoothie base into a bowl. Arrange the air-fried berries and nuts on top.
6. **Enjoy!** Feel free to add additional toppings like unsweetened shredded coconut, cocoa nibs, or a drizzle of keto-friendly syrup.

Nutritional Information (Per Serving): Calories: 550, Protein: 25g, Carbohydrates: 15g, Fats: 40g, Fiber: 10g, Cholesterol: 100mg, Sodium: 200mg, Potassium: 500mg

10.1 Air Fryer Keto Chia Seed Pudding

Yield: 2 servings **Prep Time:** 10 minutes **Soak Time:** 4-6 hours (or overnight) **Cook Time:** 5-7 minutes (for toppings)

Ingredients:

For the Chia Seed Pudding:

- 1/2 cup chia seeds
- 1 cup unsweetened almond milk
- 1/4 cup heavy cream
- 2 tablespoons unsweetened almond butter
- 1 tablespoon vanilla extract
- 1/4 teaspoon cinnamon
- Pinch of salt
- Optional: 1-2 tablespoons sweetener (erythritol, stevia) to taste

For the Air-Fried Toppings:

- 1/4 cup chopped walnuts or pecans
- 1/4 cup unsweetened shredded coconut
- 1 tablespoon coconut oil

Instructions:

1. **Prepare the chia seed pudding:** In a jar or container, whisk together the chia seeds, almond milk, heavy cream, almond butter, vanilla extract, cinnamon, salt, and optional sweetener. To prevent clumps, whisk the chia seed mixture vigorously when preparing the pudding.
2. **Soak the pudding:** Cover the container and refrigerate for at least 4-6 hours, or overnight, until the pudding has thickened.
3. **Prepare the air fryer:** Preheat your air fryer to 350°F (175°C).
4. **Air fry the toppings:** Toss the chopped nuts and shredded coconut with 1 tablespoon of coconut oil. Spread the mixture in a single layer in the air fryer basket. Cook for 5-7 minutes, shaking the basket halfway through, until the nuts are lightly toasted and the coconut is golden brown.

5. **Assemble the pudding:** Divide the chia seed pudding into two bowls. Top each with the air-fried nuts and coconut.
6. **Enjoy!** Feel free to add additional toppings like sliced berries, a drizzle of keto-friendly chocolate syrup, or a sprinkle of cinnamon.

Nutritional Information (Per Serving): Calories: 400, Protein: 15g, Carbohydrates: 10g, Fats: 30g, Fiber: 10g, Cholesterol: 50mg, Sodium: 150mg, Potassium: 300mg

11.1 Crispy Keto French Toast Sticks

Yield: 4 servings **Prep Time:** 10 minutes **Cook Time:** 5-7 minutes

Ingredients:

- 4 slices keto-friendly bread (almond flour, coconut flour, or other low-carb bread)
- 2 large eggs
- 1/4 cup heavy cream
- 1 tablespoon melted butter
- 1/4 teaspoon cinnamon
- 1/8 teaspoon nutmeg
- 1/4 teaspoon vanilla extract
- Pinch of salt
- Optional: 1-2 tablespoons sweetener (erythritol, stevia) to taste
- Optional: 1/4 cup chopped nuts (almonds, pecans) for topping

Instructions:

1. **Prepare the custard mixture:** In a shallow dish, whisk together the eggs, heavy cream, melted butter, cinnamon, nutmeg, vanilla extract, salt, and optional sweetener.
2. **Soak the bread:** Dip each slice of bread into the custard mixture, ensuring both sides are fully coated.
3. **Prepare the air fryer:** Preheat your air fryer to 375°F (190°C).
4. **Air fry the French toast sticks:** Place the soaked bread slices in the air fryer basket, making sure they are not overlapping. Cook for 5-7 minutes, flipping halfway through, until golden brown and crispy.
5. **Top and serve:** Immediately sprinkle the French toast sticks with chopped nuts, if desired. Serve warm with a side of keto-friendly syrup or whipped cream.
- whipped cream.

Nutritional Information (Per Serving): Calories: 250, Protein: 10g, Carbohydrates: 5g, Fats: 18g, Fiber: 2g, Cholesterol: 150mg, Sodium: 150mg, Potassium: 100mg

1.2 Juicy Keto Air Fryer Chicken Breast
Yield: 2 servings **Prep Time:** 5 minutes **Cook Time:** 12-15 minutes

ngredients:

- 2 boneless, skinless chicken breasts (about 6 ounces each)
- 1 tablespoon olive oil
- 1/2 teaspoon salt
- 1/4 teaspoon black pepper
- 1/4 teaspoon garlic powder
- 1/4 teaspoon onion powder
- Optional: 1/4 teaspoon paprika
- Optional: 1/4 teaspoon dried oregano

nstructions:

1. **Prepare the chicken:** Pat the chicken breasts dry with paper towels.
2. **Season the chicken:** In a small bowl, combine the olive oil, salt, pepper, garlic powder, onion powder, and optional spices. Rub the mixture all over the chicken breasts.
3. **Air fry:** Preheat your air fryer to 400°F (200°C). Place the seasoned chicken breasts in the air fryer basket, making sure they are not overlapping. Cook for 12-15 minutes, flipping halfway through, until the internal temperature reaches 165°F (74°C). You can use a meat thermometer to check the temperature.
4. **Rest:** Let the chicken breasts rest for 5 minutes before slicing and serving.

utritional Information (Per Serving): Calories: 200, Protein: 30g, Carbohydrates: 0g, Fats: 7g, Fiber: 0g, holesterol: 80mg, Sodium: 150mg, Potassium: 300mg

2.2 Crispy Keto Salmon with Lemon Herb Butter
Yield: 2 servings **Prep Time:** 5 minutes **Cook Time:** 8-10 minutes

gredients:

- 2 salmon fillets (about 6 ounces each)
- 1 tablespoon olive oil
- 1/2 teaspoon salt
- 1/4 teaspoon black pepper
- 1 tablespoon butter
- 1 tablespoon lemon juice
- 1 tablespoon chopped fresh parsley
- 1/4 teaspoon garlic powder
- 1/4 teaspoon dried dill

structions:

1. **Prepare the salmon:** Pat the salmon fillets dry with paper towels.
2. **Season the salmon:** In a small bowl, combine the olive oil, salt, and pepper. Rub the mixture all over the salmon fillets.
3. **Air fry:** Preheat your air fryer to 400°F (200°C). Place the seasoned salmon fillets in the air fryer basket, making sure they are not overlapping. Cook for 8-10 minutes, or until the salmon is cooked through and flakes easily with a fork. You can use a meat thermometer to check the internal temperature, which should reach 145°F (63°C).
4. **Prepare the lemon herb butter:** While the salmon is cooking, melt the butter in a small saucepan over low heat. Add the lemon juice, parsley, garlic powder, and dill. Stir until combined.
5. **Serve:** Remove the salmon from the air fryer and drizzle with the lemon herb butter. Serve immediately.

Nutritional Information (Per Serving): Calories: 350, Protein: 30g, Carbohydrates: 1g, Fats: 25g, Fiber: 1g, Cholesterol: 150mg, Sodium: 200mg, Potassium: 400mg

3.2 Easy Keto Ground Beef Stir-Fry
Yield: 2 servings **Prep Time:** 10 minutes **Cook Time:** 10-12 minutes

Ingredients:

- 1 pound ground beef
- 1 tablespoon olive oil
- 1/2 cup chopped onion
- 1 cup chopped broccoli florets
- 1 cup chopped bell peppers (any color)
- 1/4 cup chopped mushrooms
- 1/4 teaspoon salt
- 1/8 teaspoon black pepper
- 1/4 teaspoon garlic powder
- 1/4 teaspoon onion powder
- Optional: 1 tablespoon soy sauce (low sodium) or tamari
- Optional: 1 tablespoon sriracha sauce

Instructions:

1. **Prepare the ground beef:** In a medium bowl, combine the ground beef, salt, pepper, garlic powder, and onion powder. Mix well.
2. **Air fry the ground beef:** Preheat your air fryer to 400°F (200°C). Add the seasoned ground beef to the air fryer basket, breaking it up into smaller pieces with a fork. Cook for 6-8 minutes, stirring halfway through, until the beef is browned and cooked through.
3. **Prepare the vegetables:** While the ground beef is cooking, heat a large skillet or wok over medium heat. Add the olive oil and sauté the onions, broccoli, bell peppers, and mushrooms for 5-7 minutes, or until the vegetables are slightly softened.
4. **Combine the ingredients:** Remove the cooked ground beef from the air fryer and add it to the skillet with the vegetables. Toss everything together until well combined.
5. **Season and serve:** Add the optional soy sauce or tamari and sriracha sauce, if desired. Stir well and serve immediately.
6. **Nutritional Information (Per Serving):** Calories: 400, Protein: 35g, Carbohydrates: 5g, Fats: 20g, Fiber: 5g, Cholesterol: 100mg, Sodium: 250mg, Potassium: 500mg

4.2 Keto Air Fryer Pizza Bites
Yield: 12 pizza bites **Prep Time:** 10 minutes **Cook Time:** 5-7 minutes

Ingredients:

- 1 cup shredded mozzarella cheese
- 1/4 cup grated parmesan cheese
- 1/4 cup almond flour
- 1 egg
- 1/4 teaspoon Italian seasoning
- 1/4 teaspoon garlic powder
- Pinch of salt
- Pinch of black pepper
- 1/4 cup pizza sauce (keto-friendly)
- 1/4 cup chopped pepperoni (optional)
- 1/4 cup chopped mushrooms (optional)
- 1/4 cup chopped bell peppers (optional)

Instructions:

1. **Prepare the dough:** In a medium bowl, combine the mozzarella cheese, parmesan cheese, almond flour, egg, Italian seasoning, garlic powder, salt, and pepper. Mix well until a dough forms.
2. **Shape the pizza bites:** Divide the dough into 12 equal portions. Roll each portion into a ball and flatten it slightly, creating a small pizza base.
3. **Add toppings:** Spread a thin layer of pizza sauce on each pizza base. Top with pepperoni, mushrooms, bell peppers, or any other desired toppings.
4. **Air fry:** Preheat your air fryer to 400°F (200°C). Place the pizza bites in the air fryer basket, making sure they are not overlapping. Cook for 5-7 minutes, or until the crust is golden brown and the cheese is melted and bubbly. You may need to shake the basket halfway through cooking to ensure even cooking.
5. **Serve:** Let the pizza bites cool slightly before serving.

Nutritional Information (Per Serving): Calories: 150, Protein: 8g, Carbohydrates: 3g, Fats: 10g, Fiber: 1g, Cholesterol: 40mg, Sodium: 150mg, Potassium: 50mg

5.2 Flavorful Keto Meatloaf

Yield: 4 servings **Prep Time:** 10 minutes **Cook Time:** 20-25 minutes

Ingredients:

- 1 pound ground beef (or a mix of ground beef and ground pork)
- 1/2 cup finely chopped onion
- 1/4 cup chopped celery
- 2 eggs
- 1/4 cup grated Parmesan cheese
- 1/4 cup almond flour
- 2 tablespoons tomato paste
- 1 tablespoon Worcestershire sauce
- 1 teaspoon dried oregano
- 1/2 teaspoon salt
- 1/4 teaspoon black pepper
- 1/4 cup keto-friendly ketchup for glazing (optional)

Instructions:

1. **Preheat the air fryer:** Set your air fryer to 375°F (190°C).
2. **Combine ingredients:** In a large bowl, combine the ground beef, onion, celery, eggs, Parmesan cheese, almond flour, tomato paste, Worcestershire sauce, oregano, salt, and pepper. Mix thoroughly with your hands until well combined.
3. **Form the meatloaf:** Shape the mixture into a loaf and place it in a lightly greased air fryer-safe baking dish or directly into the air fryer basket.
4. **Air fry the meatloaf:** Cook for 20-25 minutes, or until the internal temperature reaches 160°F (71°C).
5. **Optional glaze:** During the last 5-10 minutes of cooking, brush the meatloaf with keto-friendly ketchup for a flavorful glaze.
6. **Rest and serve:** Allow the meatloaf to rest for a few minutes before slicing and serving.

Nutritional Information (per serving): Calories: 350, Protein: 25g, Carbohydrates: 3g, Fats: 20g, Fiber: 2g, Cholesterol: 100mg, Sodium: 400mg, Potassium: 400mg

6.2 Creamy Keto Chicken Parmesan
Yield: 2 servings **Prep Time:** 10 minutes **Cook Time:** 15-20 minutes

Ingredients:

- **Chicken:**
    - 2 boneless, skinless chicken breasts (about 6 ounces each)
    - 1/4 cup grated Parmesan cheese
    - 1/4 cup almond flour
    - 1/2 teaspoon dried oregano
    - 1/4 teaspoon garlic powder
    - 1/4 teaspoon salt
    - 1/4 teaspoon black pepper

- **Sauce:**
    - 1/2 cup marinara sauce (keto-friendly)
    - 1/4 cup heavy cream
    - 1 tablespoon grated Parmesan cheese
    - 1/4 teaspoon dried oregano
    - 1/4 teaspoon garlic powder
    - 1/4 teaspoon salt
    - 1/4 teaspoon black pepper

- **Optional Toppings:**
    - 1/4 cup shredded mozzarella cheese
    - Fresh basil leaves

Instructions:

1. **Prepare the chicken:** Preheat your air fryer to 400°F (200°C). Lightly spray the air fryer basket with cooking spray. In a shallow dish, combine the Parmesan cheese, almond flour, oregano, garlic powder, salt, and pepper. Dip each chicken breast into the mixture, ensuring it's fully coated.
2. **Air fry the chicken:** Place the coated chicken breasts in the air fryer basket. Cook for 10-12 minutes, flipping halfway through cooking, until golden brown and cooked through. The internal temperature should reach 165°F (74°C).
3. **Make the sauce:** While the chicken is cooking, combine the marinara sauce, heavy cream, Parmesan cheese, oregano, garlic powder, salt, and pepper in a small saucepan. Bring to a simmer over medium heat, stirring occasionally, until thickened.
4. **Assemble the chicken Parmesan:** Transfer the cooked chicken breasts to a baking dish or serving plate. Pour the sauce over the chicken, ensuring it's evenly coated.
5. **Optional toppings:** Top with shredded mozzarella cheese and fresh basil leaves.
6. **Broil (optional):** If desired, broil the chicken Parmesan for 1-2 minutes, or until the cheese is melted and slightly browned.
7. **Serve immediately:** Enjoy hot with a side of cauliflower rice, zucchini noodles, or a green salad.

Nutritional Information (per serving): Calories: 450, Protein: 30g, Carbohydrates: 10g, Fats: 25g, Fiber: 3g, Cholesterol: 100mg, Sodium: 400mg, Potassium: 300mg

7.2 Keto Shepherd's Pie with Cauliflower Mash
Yield: 4 servings **Prep Time:** 15 minutes **Cook Time:** 20-25 minutes

ngredients:

- **Filling:**

  - 1 pound ground beef
  - 1/2 cup chopped onion
  - 1/4 cup chopped celery
  - 1 teaspoon dried thyme
  - 1/2 teaspoon salt
  - 1/4 teaspoon black pepper
  - 1/2 cup beef broth
  - 1/4 cup tomato paste
  - 1 tablespoon Worcestershire sauce

- **Cauliflower Mash:**

  - 1 large head cauliflower, chopped into florets
  - 1/4 cup heavy cream
  - 2 tablespoons butter
  - 1/4 teaspoon salt
  - 1/4 teaspoon black pepper
  - 1/4 teaspoon garlic powder (optional)
  - 1/4 cup grated Parmesan cheese (optional)

nstructions:

1. **Prepare the filling:** Preheat your air fryer to 375°F (190°C). In a large skillet, brown the ground beef over medium heat, breaking it up with a spoon. Drain off any excess fat. Add the onion, celery, thyme, salt, and pepper to the skillet and cook until softened, about 5 minutes. Stir in the beef broth, tomato paste, and Worcestershire sauce. Simmer for 5 minutes, or until the sauce has thickened slightly.
2. **Prepare the cauliflower mash:** While the filling is simmering, place the cauliflower florets in a steamer basket or a saucepan with a few inches of water. Steam until tender, about 10-15 minutes. Drain the cauliflower and transfer it to a food processor or blender. Add the heavy cream, butter, salt, pepper, garlic powder (optional), and Parmesan cheese (optional). Process until smooth and creamy.
3. **Assemble the shepherd's pie:** Pour the meat filling into a greased 8-inch square baking dish or an air fryer-safe casserole dish. Top with the cauliflower mash, spreading it evenly over the filling.
4. **Air fry the shepherd's pie:** Place the dish in the preheated air fryer. Cook for 15-20 minutes, or until the cauliflower mash is golden brown and heated through.
5. **Rest and serve:** Allow the shepherd's pie to rest for a few minutes before serving.

utritional Information (per serving): Calories: 400, Protein: 25g, Carbohydrates: 10g, Fats: 25g, Fiber: 4g, holesterol: 100mg, Sodium: 400mg, Potassium: 400mg

8.2 Air Fryer Keto Burgers with Low-Carb Buns
Yield: 4 servings **Prep Time:** 10 minutes **Cook Time:** 10-12 minutes

gredients:

- **Burgers:**

  - 1 pound ground beef (80/20 or 90/10)
  - 1/4 cup finely chopped onion
  - 1/4 teaspoon garlic powder
  - 1/4 teaspoon salt
  - 1/4 teaspoon black pepper
  - 1/4 teaspoon Worcestershire sauce

- **Low-Carb Buns:**
  - 4 low-carb burger buns (e.g., almond flour, coconut flour, or lettuce wraps)
- **Toppings:**

  - 4 slices cheese (e.g., cheddar, Swiss, or provolone)
  - 1/2 cup chopped lettuce
  - 1/4 cup diced tomato
  - 1/4 cup sliced pickles
  - 1/4 cup red onion, thinly sliced
  - 2 tablespoons mayonnaise
  - 1 tablespoon ketchup (keto-friendly)
  - Hot sauce, to taste

Instructions:

1. **Prepare the burgers:** In a large bowl, combine the ground beef, onion, garlic powder, salt, pepper, and Worcestershire sauce. Mix gently with your hands until well combined, but avoid overmixing. Form the mixture into 4 patties, about 1/2 inch thick.
2. **Preheat the air fryer:** Set your air fryer to 400°F (200°C). Lightly spray the air fryer basket with cooking spray.
3. **Air fry the burgers:** Place the patties in the air fryer basket, leaving a little space between each one. Cook for 6-8 minutes, flipping halfway through cooking, until cooked to your desired doneness. The internal temperature should reach 160°F (71°C) for medium-well.
4. **Toast the buns:** While the burgers are cooking, warm the low-carb buns according to their package instructions. You can also lightly toast them in the air fryer for a few minutes for a crispier texture.
5. **Assemble the burgers:** Place a cooked burger patty on each toasted bun. Top with cheese, lettuce, tomato, pickles, red onion, mayonnaise, ketchup, and hot sauce.

Nutritional Information (per serving): Calories: 450, Protein: 30g, Carbohydrates: 10g, Fats: 25g, Fiber: 4g, Cholesterol: 100mg, Sodium: 400mg, Potassium: 400mg

9.2 Keto Air Fryer Stuffed Peppers
Yield: 4 servings **Prep Time:** 20 minutes **Cook Time:** 25-30 minutes

Ingredients:

- **Peppers:**
  - 4 bell peppers (any color), halved and seeded
- **Filling:**
  - 1 pound ground beef (80/20 or 90/10)
  - 1/2 cup chopped onion
  - 1/2 cup chopped green bell pepper
  - 1/2 cup chopped red bell pepper
  - 1/4 cup chopped celery
  - 1/4 cup shredded cheddar cheese (optional)
  - 1 egg
  - 1/4 cup heavy cream
  - 1 teaspoon garlic powder
  - 1/2 teaspoon salt
  - 1/4 teaspoon black pepper

- **Sauce:**
  - 1/2 cup marinara sauce (keto-friendly)
  - 1/4 cup water
  - 1 teaspoon dried oregano

Instructions:

1. **Prepare the peppers:** Preheat your air fryer to 400°F (200°C). Remove the tops and seeds from the bell peppers and place them in the air fryer basket. Air fry for 5 minutes, or until slightly softened.

2. **Make the filling:** While the peppers are air frying, brown the ground beef in a large skillet over medium heat. Drain off any excess fat. Add the chopped onion, green bell pepper, red bell pepper, and celery to the skillet and cook until softened, about 5 minutes. Remove from heat and let cool slightly.
3. **Combine and stuff the peppers:** In a large bowl, combine the cooled beef mixture, cheddar cheese (optional), egg, heavy cream, garlic powder, salt, and black pepper. Mix well. Fill the softened bell peppers with the meat mixture, mounding slightly.
4. **Make the sauce:** In a small bowl, whisk together the marinara sauce, water, and oregano. Pour the sauce over the stuffed peppers.
5. **Air fry the stuffed peppers:** Place the stuffed peppers in the air fryer basket and air fry for 20-25 minutes, or until the peppers are tender and the filling is cooked through.
6. **Serve immediately:** Enjoy the hot, cheesy keto air fryer stuffed peppers with a side of your favorite keto-friendly vegetables or salad.

Nutritional Information (per serving): Calories: 350, Protein: 25g, Carbohydrates: 10g, Fats: 25g, Fiber: 5g, Cholesterol: 100mg, Sodium: 500mg, Potassium: 400mg

10.2 Creamy Keto Chicken Alfredo with Zucchini Noodles
Yield: 2 servings **Prep Time:** 15 minutes **Cook Time:** 15-20 minutes

Ingredients:
- **Chicken:**
  - 2 boneless, skinless chicken breasts (about 6 ounces each)
  - 1/2 teaspoon garlic powder
  - 1/4 teaspoon salt
  - 1/4 teaspoon black pepper
- **Zucchini Noodles:**
  - 2 medium zucchini, spiralized
  - 1 tablespoon olive oil
- **Alfredo Sauce:**
  - 1/2 cup heavy cream
  - 1/4 cup grated Parmesan cheese
  - 2 tablespoons butter
  - 1/4 teaspoon garlic powder
  - 1/4 teaspoon salt
  - 1/4 teaspoon black pepper
  - 1/4 teaspoon nutmeg (optional)
- **Optional Toppings:**
  - Fresh parsley, chopped
  - Red pepper flakes

Instructions:

1. **Prepare the chicken:** Preheat your air fryer to 400°F (200°C). In a bowl, combine the chicken breasts with garlic powder, salt, and pepper.
2. **Air fry the chicken:** Place the seasoned chicken breasts in the air fryer basket and cook for 10-12 minutes, flipping halfway through, until cooked through. The internal temperature should reach 165°F (74°C).
3. **Prepare the zucchini noodles:** While the chicken is cooking, toss the zucchini noodles with olive oil in a bowl. Spread the noodles in a single layer on a baking sheet lined with parchment paper.
4. **Air fry the zucchini noodles:** Place the baking sheet in the air fryer. Air fry for 5-7 minutes, flipping halfway through, until the zucchini noodles are slightly softened and browned.
5. **Make the Alfredo sauce:** While the zucchini noodles are cooking, melt the butter in a saucepan over medium heat. Whisk in the heavy cream, Parmesan cheese, garlic powder, salt, pepper, and nutmeg (optional). Cook, stirring constantly, until the sauce thickens slightly.
6. **Assemble the dish:** Remove the cooked chicken from the air fryer and slice it into bite-sized pieces. Divide the zucchini noodles between two plates. Top with the sliced chicken and pour the Alfredo sauce over the top.
7. **Serve immediately:** Garnish with fresh parsley and red pepper flakes (optional) and enjoy hot.

Nutritional Information (per serving): Calories: 500, Protein: 30g, Carbohydrates: 10g, Fats: 30g, Fiber: 4g, Cholesterol: 100mg, Sodium: 400mg, Potassium: 400mg

11.2 Keto Beef & Broccoli Stir-Fry
Yield: 2 servings **Prep Time:** 10 minutes **Cook Time:** 10-12 minutes

Ingredients:

- **Beef:**
  - 1/2 pound sirloin steak, cut into thin strips
  - 1 tablespoon soy sauce
  - 1 tablespoon sesame oil
  - 1/2 teaspoon garlic powder
  - 1/4 teaspoon black pepper
- **Broccoli:**
  - Air Fryer Keto Chia Seed Pudding,14
  - 1 head broccoli, cut into florets
  - 1 tablespoon olive oil
- **Sauce:**
  - 1/4 cup low-sodium chicken broth
  - 1 tablespoon soy sauce
  - 1 tablespoon rice vinegar
  - 1 teaspoon honey (optional, use sugar-free alternative)
  - 1/2 teaspoon sesame oil
  - 1/4 teaspoon garlic powder
  - 1/4 teaspoon red pepper flakes (optional)

Instructions:

1. **Prepare the beef:** In a bowl, combine the beef strips with soy sauce, sesame oil, garlic powder, and black pepper. Toss to coat evenly.
2. **Prepare the broccoli:** In a separate bowl, toss the broccoli florets with olive oil.
3. **Air fry the beef:** Preheat your air fryer to 400°F (200°C). Place the marinated beef in the air fryer basket and cook for 5-7 minutes, shaking the basket halfway through cooking, until cooked through and slightly browned.
4. **Air fry the broccoli:** While the beef is cooking, place the broccoli in the air fryer basket and cook for 5-7 minutes, shaking the basket halfway through cooking, until tender and slightly crispy.
5. **Make the sauce:** In a small saucepan, combine the chicken broth, soy sauce, rice vinegar, sesame oil, garlic powder, and red pepper flakes (optional). Bring to a simmer over medium heat, stirring constantly, until slightly thickened.
6. **Assemble the stir-fry:** Remove the cooked beef and broccoli from the air fryer. Combine the beef, broccoli and sauce in a large bowl and toss to coat evenly.

Nutritional Information (per serving): Calories: 400, Protein: 30g, Carbohydrates: 10g, Fats: 20g, Fiber: 4g, Cholesterol: 100mg, Sodium: 400mg, Potassium: 400mg

12.2 Keto Chicken Salad with Avocado Dressing

Yield: 2 servings **Prep time:** 10 minutes **Cook time:** 10-12 minutes

Ingredients:

For the chicken:

- 1 boneless, skinless chicken breast
- 1/2 teaspoon salt
- 1/4 teaspoon black pepper
- 1 tablespoon olive oil

For the avocado dressing:

- 1 ripe avocado, mashed
- 1 tablespoon mayonnaise
- 1 tablespoon lemon juice\
- 1/4 teaspoon garlic powder
- 1/4 teaspoon onion powder
- Salt and pepper to taste

For the salad:

- 1 cup cooked chicken, shredded
- 1/4 cup chopped celery
- 1/4 cup chopped red onion
- 1/4 cup chopped walnuts (optional)
- 1/4 cup chopped fresh parsley
- Salt and pepper to taste

Instructions:

1. **Air fry the chicken:** Preheat your air fryer to 400°F (200°C). Season the chicken breast with salt and pepper. Drizzle with olive oil and place in the air fryer basket. Cook for 10-12 minutes, flipping halfway through, until the chicken is cooked through and no longer pink. Let the chicken rest for a few minutes before shredding it.
2. **Make the avocado dressing:** In a small bowl, combine the mashed avocado, mayonnaise, lemon juice, garlic powder, onion powder, salt, and pepper. Mix well until smooth.
3. **Assemble the salad:** In a large bowl, combine the shredded chicken, chopped celery, red onion, walnuts (if using), and chopped parsley. Pour the avocado dressing over the chicken salad and toss gently to coat.
4. **Serve:** Divide the chicken salad between two plates and enjoy!

Nutritional Information (per serving): Calories: 550, Protein: 35g Carbohydrates: 10g, Fats: 35g, Fiber: 5g, Cholesterol: 80mg, Sodium: 400mg, Potassium: 500mg

3. Snacks & Sides:

1.3 Crispy Keto Zucchini Fries
Yield: 4 servings **Prep Time:** 10 minutes **Cook Time:** 10-12 minutes

Ingredients:

- 2 medium zucchini, sliced into 1/4-inch thick fries
- 2 tablespoons olive oil
- 1/4 cup grated Parmesan cheese
- 1/2 teaspoon garlic powder
- 1/4 teaspoon salt
- 1/4 teaspoon black pepper
- 1/4 teaspoon dried oregano (optional)

Instructions:

1. **Prepare the zucchini:** Preheat your air fryer to 400°F (200°C). In a large bowl, toss the zucchini fries with olive oil, Parmesan cheese, garlic powder, salt, pepper, and oregano (optional). Make sure each fry is evenly coated.
2. **Air fry the zucchini fries:** Place the coated zucchini fries in the air fryer basket, ensuring they are not overcrowding. Air fry for 8-10 minutes, shaking the basket halfway through cooking, until the fries are tend and slightly crispy.
3. **Serve immediately:** Enjoy the warm, crispy zucchini fries as a healthy snack, side dish, or topping for keto-friendly meals.

Nutritional Information (per serving): Calories: 150, Protein: 3g, Carbohydrates: 7g, Fats: 10g, Fiber: 2g, Cholesterol: 10mg, Sodium: 200mg, Potassium: 300mg

2.3 Cheesy Keto Cauliflower Bites
Yield: 4 servings **Prep Time:** 10 minutes **Cook Time:** 10-12 minutes

Ingredients:

- 1 head cauliflower, cut into small florets (about 2 cups)
- 1/4 cup grated Parmesan cheese
- 1/4 cup shredded mozzarella cheese
- 2 tablespoons melted butter
- 1 teaspoon garlic powder
- 1/4 teaspoon salt
- 1/4 teaspoon black pepper
- 1/4 teaspoon dried oregano (optional)

Instructions:

1. **Prepare the cauliflower:** Preheat your air fryer to 400°F (200°C). In a large bowl, combine the cauliflower florets, Parmesan cheese, mozzarella cheese, melted butter, garlic powder, salt, pepper, and oregano (optional). Toss to coat evenly.
2. **Air fry the cauliflower bites:** Place the coated cauliflower florets in the air fryer basket, ensuring they are not overcrowding. Air fry for 8-10 minutes, shaking the basket halfway through cooking, until the bites are tender and slightly crispy.
3. **Serve immediately:** Enjoy the warm, cheesy cauliflower bites as a healthy snack, side dish, or topping for keto-friendly meals.

Nutritional Information (per serving): Calories: 170, Protein: 5g, Carbohydrates: 6g, Fats: 12g, Fiber: 2g, Cholesterol: 20mg, Sodium: 250mg, Potassium: 250mg

3.3 Keto Air Fryer Onion Rings
Yield: 4 servings **Prep Time:** 15 minutes **Cook Time:** 10-12 minutes

Ingredients:

- 1 large onion, sliced into 1/2-inch thick rings
- 1/4 cup almond flour
- 1/4 cup grated Parmesan cheese
- 1/4 cup melted butter
- 1 teaspoon garlic powder
- 1/2 teaspoon salt
- 1/4 teaspoon black pepper
- 1/4 teaspoon dried thyme (optional)
- 1 egg, beaten (optional)

Instructions:

1. **Prepare the onion rings:** Preheat your air fryer to 400°F (200°C). In a shallow dish, combine the almond flour, Parmesan cheese, melted butter, garlic powder, salt, pepper, and thyme (optional).
2. **Coat the onion rings:** If using the egg, dip each onion ring in the beaten egg before coating it in the almond flour mixture. If omitting the egg, simply coat the onion rings directly in the almond flour mixture, ensuring they are evenly coated.
3. **Air fry the onion rings:** Place the coated onion rings in the air fryer basket, ensuring they are not overcrowding. Air fry for 8-10 minutes, shaking the basket halfway through cooking, until the onion rings are golden brown and crispy.
4. **Serve immediately:** Enjoy the warm, crispy onion rings as a healthy snack, side dish, or topping for keto-friendly meals.

Nutritional Information (per serving): Calories: 180, Protein: 4g, Carbohydrates: 6g, Fats: 14g, Fiber: 2g, Cholesterol: 20mg, Sodium: 200mg, Potassium: 200mg

4.3 Keto Avocado Fries
Yield: 4 servings **Prep Time:** 10 minutes **Cook Time:** 8-10 minutes

Ingredients:

- 2 ripe avocados, halved and pitted
- 1/4 cup almond flour
- 1/4 cup grated Parmesan cheese
- 2 tablespoons melted coconut oil
- 1 teaspoon garlic powder
- 1/2 teaspoon salt
- 1/4 teaspoon black pepper
- 1/4 teaspoon paprika (optional)

Instructions:

1. **Prepare the avocado fries:** Preheat your air fryer to 400°F (200°C). Using a sharp knife, slice each avocado half lengthwise into 1/2-inch thick fries.
2. **Coat the avocado fries:** In a shallow dish, combine the almond flour, Parmesan cheese, melted coconut oil, garlic powder, salt, pepper, and paprika (optional). Toss the avocado fries in the mixture, ensuring they are evenly coated.
3. **Air fry the avocado fries:** Place the coated avocado fries in the air fryer basket, ensuring they are not overcrowding. Air fry for 6-8 minutes, shaking the basket halfway through cooking, until the avocado fries are golden brown and slightly crispy.

4. **Serve immediately:** Enjoy the warm, crispy avocado fries as a healthy snack, side dish, or topping for keto-friendly meals.

Nutritional Information (per serving): Calories: 160, Protein: 2g, Carbohydrates: 5g, Fats: 14g, Fiber: 3g, Cholesterol: 10mg, Sodium: 150mg, Potassium: 400mg

5.3 Air Fryer Keto Sweet Potato Fries
Yield: 4 servings **Prep Time:** 10 minutes **Cook Time:** 15-20 minutes

Ingredients:

- 1 large sweet potato, peeled and cut into 1/2-inch thick fries
- 2 tablespoons olive oil
- 1/4 cup grated Parmesan cheese
- 1 teaspoon garlic powder
- 1/2 teaspoon salt
- 1/4 teaspoon black pepper
- 1/4 teaspoon cinnamon (optional)

Instructions:

1. **Prepare the sweet potato fries:** Preheat your air fryer to 400°F (200°C). In a large bowl, combine the swee potato fries, olive oil, Parmesan cheese, garlic powder, salt, pepper, and cinnamon (optional). Toss to coat evenly.
2. **Air fry the sweet potato fries:** Place the coated sweet potato fries in the air fryer basket, ensuring they are not overcrowding. Air fry for 10-12 minutes, shaking the basket halfway through cooking, until the sweet potato fries are golden brown and slightly crispy.
3. **Serve immediately:** Enjoy the warm, crispy sweet potato fries as a healthy snack, side dish, or topping for keto-friendly meals.

Nutritional Information (per serving): Calories: 180, Protein: 3g, Carbohydrates: 15g, Fats: 10g, Fiber: 4g, Cholesterol: 10mg, Sodium: 150mg, Potassium: 500mg

6.3 Crispy Keto Green Bean Fries
Yield: 4 servings **Prep Time:** 10 minutes **Cook Time:** 10-12 minutes

Ingredients:

- 1 pound green beans, trimmed and cut into 1-inch pieces
- 2 tablespoons olive oil
- 1/4 cup grated Parmesan cheese
- 1/2 teaspoon garlic powder
- 1/4 teaspoon salt
- 1/4 teaspoon black pepper
- 1/4 teaspoon dried thyme (optional)

Instructions:

1. **Prepare the green bean fries:** Preheat your air fryer to 400°F (200°C). In a large bowl, combine the green bean pieces, olive oil, Parmesan cheese, garlic powder, salt, pepper, and thyme (optional). Toss to coat evenly.

2. **Air fry the green bean fries:** Place the coated green bean fries in the air fryer basket, ensuring they are not overcrowding. Air fry for 8-10 minutes, shaking the basket halfway through cooking, until the fries are tender and slightly crispy.
3. **Serve immediately:** Enjoy the warm, crispy green bean fries as a healthy snack, side dish, or topping for keto-friendly meals.

Nutritional Information (per serving): Calories: 130, Protein: 3g, Carbohydrates: 6g, Fats: 8g, Fiber: 4g, Cholesterol: 10mg, Sodium: 150mg, Potassium: 300mg

7.3 Air Fryer Keto Asparagus with Lemon Butter
Yield: 4 servings **Prep Time:** 10 minutes **Cook Time:** 10-12 minutes

Ingredients:

- 1 pound asparagus, trimmed
- 2 tablespoons olive oil
- 1 tablespoon lemon juice
- 1/4 cup melted butter
- 1/4 teaspoon garlic powder
- 1/4 teaspoon salt
- 1/4 teaspoon black pepper

Instructions:

1. **Prepare the asparagus:** Preheat your air fryer to 400°F (200°C). In a large bowl, combine the asparagus spears, olive oil, lemon juice, melted butter, garlic powder, salt, and pepper. Toss to coat evenly.
2. **Air fry the asparagus:** Place the coated asparagus spears in the air fryer basket, ensuring they are not overcrowding. Air fry for 8-10 minutes, shaking the basket halfway through cooking, until the asparagus is tender-crisp and slightly browned.
3. **Serve immediately:** Transfer the air fryer asparagus to a serving dish and enjoy

Nutritional Information (per serving): Calories: 120, Protein: 3g, Carbohydrates: 8g, Fats: 10g, Fiber: 3g, Cholesterol: 10mg, Sodium: 150mg, Potassium: 300mg

8.3 Keto Cheese Curds
Yield: 4 servings **Prep time:** 5 minutes **Cook time:** 5-7 minutes

Ingredients:

- 1 cup (250g) fresh cheese curds
- 2 tablespoons melted butter
- 1 tablespoon lemon juice
- 1/4 teaspoon garlic powder (optional)
- Salt and black pepper to taste
- Fresh parsley or chives for garnish (optional)\

Instructions:

1. **Prepare the cheese curds:** In a bowl, combine the cheese curds with the melted butter, lemon juice, and garlic powder (if using). Toss gently to coat the cheese curds evenly.
2. **Preheat the air fryer:** Set your air fryer to 400°F (200°C) and allow it to preheat for 3-5 minutes.

3. **Cook the cheese curds:** Carefully add the coated cheese curds to the air fryer basket, ensuring they are in a single layer. Cook for 5-7 minutes, shaking the basket every 2-3 minutes to ensure even cooking.
4. **Check for doneness:** The cheese curds are ready when they are golden brown and crispy.
5. **Serve immediately:** Transfer the cooked cheese curds to a serving plate and sprinkle with salt, pepper, and fresh herbs (if desired). Serve warm with your favorite keto-friendly dipping sauce, like avocado crema or a spicy keto ranch dressing.

Nutritional Information (per serving): Calories: 250, Protein: 15g, Carbohydrates: 2g, Fats: 20g, Fiber: 0g, Cholesterol: 70mg, Sodium: 300mg, Potassium: 100mg

9.3 Spicy Keto Buffalo Cauliflower Wings
Yield: 4 servings **Prep time:** 10 minutes **Cook time:** 15-20 minutes

Ingredients:

- 1 head cauliflower, cut into bite-sized florets
- 2 tablespoons olive oil
- 1/2 teaspoon salt
- 1/4 teaspoon black pepper
- 1/4 cup hot sauce (your favorite buffalo sauce)
- 2 tablespoons melted butter
- 1 tablespoon vinegar (apple cider or white vinegar)
- 1/4 teaspoon garlic powder (optional)
- 1/4 teaspoon onion powder (optional)
- 1/4 cup crumbled blue cheese (optional)
- Fresh celery sticks and carrot sticks (optional) for dipping

Instructions:

1. **Prepare the cauliflower:** Preheat your air fryer to 400°F (200°C). In a large bowl, toss the cauliflower florets with olive oil, salt, and pepper.
2. **Air fry the cauliflower:** Arrange the cauliflower florets in a single layer in the air fryer basket. Cook for 10-12 minutes, shaking the basket halfway through to ensure even browning.
3. **Make the buffalo sauce:** In a small bowl, whisk together the hot sauce, melted butter, vinegar, garlic powder, and onion powder (if using).
4. **Toss in the sauce:** Once the cauliflower florets are cooked, transfer them back to the bowl and toss with the buffalo sauce until evenly coated.
5. **Air fry again:** Return the coated cauliflower to the air fryer basket and cook for an additional 2-4 minutes, until the sauce is slightly thickened and the florets are crispy.
6. **Serve:** Transfer the cauliflower wings to a serving platter and garnish with crumbled blue cheese (optional). Serve with fresh celery and carrot sticks for dipping.

Nutritional Information (per serving): Calories: 280, Protein: 6g, Carbohydrates: 7g, Fats: 20g, Fiber: 4g, Cholesterol: 25mg, Sodium: 400mg, Potassium: 300mg

10.3 Keto Pickles with Dill & Garlic
Yield: 4 servings **Prep time:** 5 minutes **Cook time:** 10-12 minutes

Ingredients:

- 1 cup (250g) dill pickle spears (choose pickles with less sugar or no added sugar)
- 2 tablespoons olive oil
- 1 tablespoon chopped fresh dill
- 2 cloves garlic, minced
- 1/2 teaspoon salt

- 1 tablespoon apple cider vinegar
- 1/4 teaspoon black pepper

Instructions:

1. **Prepare the pickles:** Preheat your air fryer to 375°F (190°C). In a bowl, combine the pickle spears with olive oil, apple cider vinegar, chopped dill, minced garlic, salt, and pepper. Toss gently to coat the pickles evenly.
2. **Air fry the pickles:** Arrange the coated pickle spears in a single layer in the air fryer basket. Cook for 10-12 minutes, shaking the basket halfway through to ensure even cooking.
3. **Check for doneness:** The pickles are ready when they are slightly browned and crispy.
4. **Serve:** Transfer the air-fried pickles to a serving dish. Serve immediately, warm or chilled, as a delicious and keto-friendly snack or appetizer.

Nutritional Information (per serving): Calories: 80, Protein: 1g, Carbohydrates: 3g, Fats: 6g, Fiber: 1g, Cholesterol: 0mg, Sodium: 500mg, Potassium: 200mg

11.3 Air Fryer Keto Macadamia Nut Brittle
Yield: 12 servings **Prep time:** 5 minutes **Cook time:** 5-7 minutes

Ingredients:

- 1 cup (120g) macadamia nuts
- 1/4 cup (50g) unsalted butter, melted
- 1/4 cup (50g) erythritol or your preferred keto-friendly sweetener
- 1/4 teaspoon vanilla extract
- 1/4 teaspoon salt
- 1 tablespoon chopped unsweetened shredded coconut (optional)
- 1/4 teaspoon cinnamon (optional)

Instructions:

1. **Preheat the air fryer:** Set your air fryer to 350°F (175°C) and allow it to preheat for 3-5 minutes.
2. **Prepare the brittle mixture:** In a bowl, combine the melted butter, erythritol, vanilla extract, and salt. Stir until well combined.
3. **Combine with nuts:** Add the macadamia nuts to the bowl and toss to coat evenly with the butter mixture.
4. **Air fry:** Spread the macadamia nut mixture in a single layer in the air fryer basket. Cook for 5-7 minutes, shaking the basket halfway through to ensure even browning and crispness.
5. **Check for doneness:** The brittle is ready when it is golden brown and slightly hardened.
6. **Cool and break:** Remove the brittle from the air fryer and allow it to cool completely on a wire rack. Once cooled, break it into bite-sized pieces.

Nutritional Information (per serving): Calories: 150, Protein: 2g, Carbohydrates: 3g, Fats: 13g, Fiber: 1g, Cholesterol: 0mg, Sodium: 50mg, Potassium: 50mg

12.3 Keto Brussels Sprouts with Mushroom
Yield: 4 servings **Prep Time:** 10 minutes **Cook Time:** 15-18 minutes

Ingredients:

- 1 pound Brussels sprouts, trimmed and halved
- 8 ounces mushrooms, sliced
- 2 tablespoons olive oil
- 1 teaspoon garlic powder
- 1/2 teaspoon salt
- 1/4 teaspoon black pepper

- 1/4 teaspoon dried thyme (optional)

Instructions:

1. **Prepare the vegetables:** Preheat your air fryer to 400°F (200°C). In a large bowl, combine the Brussels sprouts, mushrooms, olive oil, garlic powder, salt, pepper, and thyme (optional). Toss to coat evenly.
2. **Air fry the vegetables:** Place the coated vegetables in the air fryer basket, ensuring they are not overcrowding. Air fry for 10-12 minutes, shaking the basket halfway through cooking, until the vegetables are tender and slightly browned.
3. **Serve immediately:** Enjoy the warm, flavorful Brussels sprouts with mushrooms as a healthy side dish or topping for keto-friendly meals.

Nutritional Information (per serving): Calories: 120, Protein: 4g, Carbohydrates: 10g, Fats: 8g, Fiber: 4g, Cholesterol: 10mg, Sodium: 150mg, Potassium: 300mg

13.3 Creamy Keto Beef and Mushroom Gravy
Yield: 4 servings **Prep Time:** 5 minutes **Cook Time:** 10-12 minutes

Ingredients:

- 1 tablespoon olive oil
- 8 ounces mushrooms, sliced
- 1/4 cup beef broth
- 1/4 cup heavy cream
- 1 tablespoon butter
- 1 teaspoon garlic powder
- 1/4 teaspoon salt
- 1/4 teaspoon black pepper
- 1/4 teaspoon dried thyme (optional)
- 1 tablespoon chopped fresh parsley (optional)

Instructions:

1. **Air fry the mushrooms:** Preheat your air fryer to 400°F (200°C). Toss the sliced mushrooms with olive oil, garlic powder, salt, pepper, and thyme (optional) in a bowl. Place the mushrooms in the air fryer basket, ensuring they are not overcrowding. Air fry for 6-8 minutes, shaking the basket halfway through cooking, until the mushrooms are tender and slightly browned.
2. **Make the gravy:** While the mushrooms are cooking, combine the beef broth, heavy cream, butter, and remaining seasonings in a saucepan. Bring to a simmer over medium heat, stirring constantly, until the butter is melted and the sauce is slightly thickened.
3. **Combine the ingredients:** Remove the mushrooms from the air fryer and add them to the saucepan with the gravy. Stir to combine.
4. **Serve the gravy:** Pour the gravy over your favorite keto-friendly dishes, such as steak, chicken, or cauliflower mash. Garnish with chopped parsley, if desired.

Nutritional Information (per serving): Calories: 150, Protein: 4g, Carbohydrates: 4g, Fats: 12g, Fiber: 2g, Cholesterol: 30mg, Sodium: 200mg, Potassium: 200mg

4. Salads
1.4 Chicken Caesar Salad with Creamy Parmesan Dressing

Yields: 4 servings **Prep Time:** 15 minutes **Cook Time:** 20 minutes

Ingredients:

Salad:

- 1.5 lbs boneless, skinless chicken breasts
- 1 tbsp olive oil
- 1 tsp salt
- 1/2 tsp black pepper
- 1 head romaine lettuce, chopped
- 1/2 cup grated Parmesan cheese
- 1/4 cup chopped fresh parsley
- 1/4 cup chopped fresh chives (optional)
- 1/4 cup croutons (optional, use keto-friendly options)

Dressing:

- 1/2 cup mayonnaise
- 1/4 cup grated Parmesan cheese
- 1 tbsp lemon juice
- 1 tbsp Dijon mustard
- 1 clove garlic, minced
- 1/2 tsp dried oregano
- 1/4 tsp salt
- 1/4 tsp black pepper

Instructions:

Chicken:

1. Preheat oven to 400°F (200°C).
2. Season chicken breasts with salt and pepper.
3. Place chicken on a baking sheet lined with parchment paper and bake for 15-20 minutes, or until internal temperature reaches 165°F (74°C).
4. Let chicken cool slightly, then shred with two forks.

Dressing:

1. Combine all dressing ingredients in a small bowl and whisk until smooth.
2. Taste and adjust seasoning as needed.

Salad:

1. In a large bowl, combine chopped romaine lettuce, shredded chicken, grated Parmesan cheese, parsley, and chives (if using).
2. Pour dressing over salad and toss to coat.
3. Add croutons (if using) and serve immediately.

Serving Suggestions:

This salad can be served as a light lunch or a hearty dinner. For a complete meal, serve it with a side of keto-friendly vegetables, such as broccoli, cauliflower, or asparagus.

Nutritional Information per Serving: Calories: 500, Protein: 35g, Carbohydrates: 5g, Fat: 30g, Fiber: 3g, Cholesterol: 100mg, Sodium: 600mg, Potassium: 500mg

2.4 Caprese Salad with Balsamic Glaze
Yield: 2 servings **Prep time:** 5 minutes **Cook time:** 5-7 minutes

Ingredients:

- 2 large tomatoes, cut into thick slices
- 1/2 cup fresh mozzarella balls, halved
- 1/4 cup fresh basil leaves
- 2 tablespoons olive oil
- 1 tablespoon balsamic vinegar
- 1 teaspoon honey or maple syrup (optional, for a sweeter glaze)
- Salt and pepper to taste
- Pinch of red pepper flakes (optional, for a spicy kick)

Instructions:

1. **Prepare the balsamic glaze:** In a small saucepan, combine the balsamic vinegar and honey (if using). Bring to a simmer over medium heat. Reduce the heat to low and cook for about 5 minutes, or until the glaze thickens slightly. Remove from heat and set aside.
2. **Preheat the air fryer:** Set your air fryer to 375°F (190°C) and allow it to preheat for 3-5 minutes.
3. **Air fry the tomatoes:** Arrange the tomato slices in a single layer in the air fryer basket. Drizzle with olive and sprinkle with salt, pepper, and red pepper flakes (if using). Air fry for 5-7 minutes, or until the tomatoes are slightly softened and warmed through.
4. **Assemble the salad:** Divide the air-fried tomato slices between two plates. Top each serving with halved mozzarella balls, fresh basil leaves, and drizzle with the balsamic glaze.

Nutritional Information (per serving): Calories: 300, Protein: 15g, Carbohydrates: 10g, Fats: 20g, Fiber: 3g, Cholesterol: 40mg, Sodium: 200mg, Potassium: 400mg

3.4 Greek Salad with Feta & Olives
Yields: 4 servings **Prep Time:** 15 minutes **Cook Time:** None

Ingredients:

- 1 head romaine lettuce, chopped
- 1 cup chopped cucumber
- 1/2 cup chopped red onion
- 1/2 cup kalamata olives, pitted and halved
- 1/2 cup crumbled feta cheese
- 1/4 cup chopped fresh dill
- 1/4 cup chopped fresh oregano
- 2 tablespoons extra virgin olive oil
- 1 tablespoon red wine vinegar
- 1 teaspoon dried oregano
- 1/2 teaspoon salt
- 1/4 teaspoon black pepper
- Optional: 1 tablespoon capers (for added brininess)

Instructions:

1. **Prepare the Salad:** In a large bowl, combine chopped romaine lettuce, cucumber, red onion, kalamata oliv feta cheese, fresh dill, and oregano.

2. **Make the Dressing:** In a small bowl, whisk together olive oil, red wine vinegar, dried oregano, salt, and pepper.
3. **Combine Salad and Dressing:** Pour the dressing over the salad and toss gently to coat.
4. **Serve:** Arrange the salad on individual plates, and top with extra feta cheese and a sprinkle of dried oregano for garnish (optional). Serve immediately.

Nutritional Information per Serving: Calories: 350, Protein: 15g, Carbohydrates: 10g, Fat: 25g, Fiber: 5g, Cholesterol: 45mg, Sodium: 400mg, Potassium: 450mg

4.4 Air Fryer Roasted Vegetable Salad
Yield: 4 servings Prep time: 10 minutes Cook time: 15-20 minutes

Ingredients:

For the roasted vegetables:

- 1 medium zucchini, diced
- 1 medium yellow squash, diced
- 1 red bell pepper, diced
- 1 cup broccoli florets
- 1/2 cup Brussels sprouts, halved

- 2 tablespoons olive oil
- 1 teaspoon Italian seasoning
- 1/2 teaspoon salt
- 1/4 teaspoon black pepper

For the avocado dressing:

- 1 ripe avocado, mashed
- 1 tablespoon mayonnaise
- 1 tablespoon lemon juice

- 1/4 teaspoon garlic powder
- 1/4 teaspoon onion powder
- Salt and pepper to taste

For the salad:

- 1/4 cup crumbled feta cheese
- 1/4 cup chopped walnuts (optional)

- 1/4 cup chopped fresh parsley

Instructions:

1. **Preheat the air fryer:** Set your air fryer to 400°F (200°C) and allow it to preheat for 3-5 minutes.
2. **Prepare the vegetables:** In a large bowl, combine the zucchini, yellow squash, bell pepper, broccoli florets, and Brussels sprouts. Toss with olive oil, Italian seasoning, salt, and pepper.
3. **Air fry the vegetables:** Spread the vegetables in a single layer in the air fryer basket. Air fry for 15-20 minutes, shaking the basket halfway through, until the vegetables are tender and slightly browned.
4. **Make the avocado dressing:** In a small bowl, combine the mashed avocado, mayonnaise, lemon juice, garlic powder, onion powder, salt, and pepper. Mix well until smooth.
5. **Assemble the salad:** Divide the roasted vegetables between four plates. Top each serving with crumbled feta cheese, chopped walnuts (if using), chopped parsley, and drizzle with the avocado dressing.

Nutritional Information (per serving): Calories: 400, Protein: 10g, Carbohydrates: 15g, Fats: 25g, Fiber: 8g, Cholesterol: 40mg, Sodium: 250mg, Potassium: 600mg

5.4 Mediterranean Salad with Lemon Herb Vinaigrette
Yield: 4 servings **Prep time:** 10 minutes **Cook time:** 10-12 minutes

Ingredients:

For the salad:

- 1 cup chopped cucumber
- 1 cup chopped red bell pepper
- 1/2 cup cherry tomatoes, halved
- 1/4 cup kalamata olives, pitted and halved

- 1/4 cup crumbled feta cheese
- 1/4 cup chopped red onion
- Fresh parsley or dill for garnish (optional)

For the lemon herb vinaigrette:

- 1/4 cup olive oil
- 2 tablespoons lemon juice
- 1 tablespoon red wine vinegar

- 1 teaspoon dried oregano
- 1/2 teaspoon dried basil
- Salt and pepper to taste

Instructions:

1. **Prepare the vinaigrette:** In a small bowl, whisk together the olive oil, lemon juice, red wine vinegar, oregano, basil, salt, and pepper until well combined.
2. **Preheat the air fryer:** Set your air fryer to 375°F (190°C) and allow it to preheat for 3-5 minutes.
3. **Air fry the vegetables:** In a bowl, combine the chopped cucumber, red bell pepper, and cherry tomatoes. Toss with a tablespoon of olive oil and a pinch of salt and pepper. Spread the vegetables in a single layer in the air fryer basket. Air fry for 10-12 minutes, shaking the basket halfway through, until the vegetables are slightly softened and warmed through.
4. **Assemble the salad:** Divide the air-fried vegetables between four plates. Top each serving with crumbled feta cheese, kalamata olives, chopped red onion, and fresh parsley or dill (if using). Drizzle with the lemon herb vinaigrette.

Nutritional Information (per serving): Calories: 350, Protein: 10g, Carbohydrates: 10g, Fats: 25g, Fiber: 5g, Cholesterol: 20mg, Sodium: 300mg, Potassium: 400mg

6.4 Easy Keto Kale Salad with Parmesan
Yields: 4 servings **Prep Time:** 15 minutes **Cook Time:** None

Ingredients:

- 1 bunch of kale, stems removed and chopped
- 1/4 cup olive oil
- 1/4 cup grated Parmesan cheese
- 1 tablespoon lemon juice
- 1 teaspoon Dijon mustard

- 1/4 teaspoon salt
- 1/4 teaspoon black pepper
- 1/4 cup chopped walnuts (optional)
- 1/4 cup sun-dried tomatoes, chopped (optional)

Instructions:

1. **Massage the Kale:** Place chopped kale in a large bowl and drizzle with olive oil. Using your hands, massage the kale for 1-2 minutes until it becomes tender and slightly wilted. This process helps break down the tough fibers in kale, making it easier to eat.

2. **Prepare the Dressing:** In a small bowl, whisk together grated Parmesan cheese, lemon juice, Dijon mustard, salt, and pepper.
3. **Combine Ingredients:** Pour the dressing over the massaged kale and toss to coat evenly.
4. **Add Toppings (Optional):** If desired, add chopped walnuts and sun-dried tomatoes to the salad. Toss gently to combine.
5. **Serve:** Serve the kale salad immediately or store it in an airtight container in the refrigerator for up to 3 days.

Nutritional Information per Serving: Calories: 250, Protein: 10g, Carbohydrates: 5g, Fat: 18g, Fiber: 4g, Cholesterol: 30mg, Sodium: 300mg, Potassium: 400mg

7.4 Tuna & Avocado Salad with Spicy Mayo & Sliced Eggs
Yields: 2 servings **Prep Time:** 15 minutes **Cook Time:** 10 minutes

Ingredients:

Salad:
- 2 cans (5 oz each) tuna in water or oil, drained
- 1 ripe avocado, diced
- 1/2 cup chopped celery
- 1/4 cup chopped red onion
- 1 tablespoon chopped fresh parsley
- 2 hard-boiled eggs, sliced

Spicy Mayo:
- 1/4 cup mayonnaise
- 1 tablespoon sriracha sauce (or more to taste)
- 1 teaspoon lemon juice
- 1/4 teaspoon salt
- 1/4 teaspoon black pepper

Optional Garnishes:
- 1 tablespoon chopped chives
- Pinch of paprika

Instructions:
1. **Prepare the Eggs:** Boil 2 eggs in a pot of water for 10 minutes. Drain and let cool in an ice bath. Peel and slice into thin rounds.
2. **Make the Spicy Mayo:** In a small bowl, combine mayonnaise, sriracha sauce, lemon juice, salt, and pepper. Whisk until well combined. Adjust the amount of sriracha to your desired level of spice.
3. **Combine Salad Ingredients:** In a medium bowl, combine drained tuna, diced avocado, chopped celery, red onion, and parsley.
4. **Assemble the Salad:** Divide the tuna salad evenly between two plates. Arrange the sliced hard-boiled eggs on top. Drizzle the spicy mayo over the salad and garnish with optional toppings like crumbled chopped chives, and a pinch of paprika.

Nutritional Information per Serving: Calories: 500, Protein: 35g, Carbohydrates: 5g, Fat: 35g, Fiber: 7g, Cholesterol: 180mg, Sodium: 600mg, Potassium: 500mg

8.4 Air Fryer Roasted Butternut Squash Salad
Yields: 2 servings **Prep time:** 10 minutes **Cook time:** 15-20 minutes

Ingredients:

- 1 small butternut squash, peeled, seeded, and cubed (about 1 1/2 cups)
- 1 tablespoon olive oil
- 1/4 teaspoon salt
- 1/8 teaspoon black pepper
- 1/4 cup crumbled feta cheese
- 1/4 cup chopped walnuts
- 2 tablespoons balsamic glaze
- Optional: 1 tablespoon chopped fresh sage or rosemary

Instructions:

1. **Prepare the squash:** Preheat the air fryer to 400°F (200°C). Toss the cubed butternut squash with olive oil, salt, and pepper in a bowl.
2. **Air fry:** Place the squash in the air fryer basket in a single layer, ensuring it's not overcrowded. Air fry for 15-20 minutes, shaking the basket halfway through to ensure even cooking. The squash should be tender and slightly caramelized.
3. **Assemble the salad:** Once cooked, transfer the butternut squash to a serving bowl. Sprinkle with feta cheese, chopped walnuts, and balsamic glaze. Garnish with fresh herbs (optional).

Nutritional Informationper serving: Calories: 300, Protein: 8g, Carbohydrates: 20g, Fats: 20g, Fiber: 5g, Cholesterol: 15mg, Sodium: 250mg, Potassium: 500mg

9.4 Keto Spinach Salad with Strawberry Vinaigrette
Yields: 2 servings **Prep time:** 5 minutes **Cook time:** 5 minutes

Ingredients:

- 1 bag (10 ounces) baby spinach
- 1/2 cup sliced strawberries
- 1/4 cup crumbled feta cheese
- 1/4 cup chopped walnuts

Strawberry Vinaigrette:

- 1/4 cup olive oil
- 2 tablespoons balsamic vinegar
- 1 tablespoon lemon juice
- 1 tablespoon maple syrup
- 1/2 teaspoon salt
- 1/4 teaspoon black pepper
- 1/4 cup chopped fresh strawberries

Instructions:

1. **Prepare the vinaigrette:** In a small bowl, whisk together the olive oil, balsamic vinegar, lemon juice, maple syrup, salt, and pepper until well combined. Stir in the chopped strawberries.
2. **Air fry the spinach:** Preheat your air fryer to 350°F (175°C). Place the spinach in the air fryer basket in a single layer, ensuring it's not overcrowded. Air fry for 3-5 minutes, or until the spinach is slightly wilted and tender.
3. **Assemble the salad:** Remove the spinach from the air fryer and transfer it to a serving bowl. Toss with the strawberries, feta cheese, and walnuts. Pour the strawberry vinaigrette over the salad and toss to coat.

Nutritional Information per serving: Calories: 350, Protein: 10g, Carbohydrates: 15g, Fats: 25g, Fiber: 4g, Cholesterol: 15mg, Sodium: 200mg, Potassium: 400mg

10.4 Mediterranean Quinoa Salad with Feta and Kalamata Olives
Yield: 4 servings **Prep time:** 15 minutes **Cook time:** 10 minutes

Ingredients:

- 1 cup cooked quinoa (substitute with cauliflower rice for a strictly keto-friendly option)
- 1/2 cup crumbled feta cheese
- 1/2 cup pitted kalamata olives, halved
- 1/4 cup chopped red onion
- 1/4 cup chopped cucumber
- 1/4 cup chopped fresh parsley

- 2 tbsp olive oil
- 1 tbsp lemon juice
- 1 tsp dried oregano
- 1/2 tsp salt
- 1/4 tsp black pepper
- Optional toppings: chopped tomatoes, red pepper flakes, crumbled toasted walnuts

Instructions:

1. **Prepare the ingredients:** Cook the quinoa according to package instructions, or prepare the cauliflower rice. Let it cool completely. Chop the onion, cucumber, and parsley.
2. **Preheat the air fryer:** Preheat your air fryer to 400°F (200°C).
3. **Air fry the quinoa (or cauliflower rice):** Place the cooked quinoa (or cauliflower rice) in the air fryer basket, spreading it out in a single layer. Cook for 5-7 minutes, shaking the basket halfway through, until lightly toasted and crispy.
4. **Combine ingredients:** In a large bowl, combine the air-fried quinoa (or cauliflower rice), crumbled feta cheese, kalamata olives, red onion, cucumber, parsley, olive oil, lemon juice, oregano, salt, and pepper. Toss to combine.
5. **Serve:** Transfer the salad to a serving bowl and garnish with your favorite toppings.

Nutritional Information (per serving): Calories: 350, Protein: 15g, Carbohydrates: 20g (10g if using cauliflower rice), Fat: 20g, Fiber: 5g, Cholesterol: 25mg, Sodium: 250mg, Potassium: 350mg

11.4 Cucumber & Dill Salad with Lemon-Herb Vinaigrette
Yields: 4 servings **Prep Time:** 15 minutes **Cook Time:** None

Ingredients:

Salad:

- 2 large cucumbers, peeled, seeded, and thinly sliced
- 1/2 cup chopped red onion
- 1/4 cup chopped fresh dill

- 1/4 cup chopped fresh parsley
- 1/4 cup crumbled feta cheese (optional)

Lemon-Herb Vinaigrette:

- 1/4 cup extra virgin olive oil
- 2 tablespoons lemon juice

- 1/2 teaspoon dried oregano
- 1/4 teaspoon salt

- 1 tablespoon red wine vinegar
- 1 teaspoon Dijon mustard
- 1/4 teaspoon black pepper

Optional Garnishes:

- 1 tablespoon chopped fresh chives
- Pinch of red pepper flakes

Instructions:

1. **Prepare the Salad:** In a large bowl, combine sliced cucumbers, red onion, chopped dill, and parsley.
2. **Make the Vinaigrette:** In a small bowl, whisk together olive oil, lemon juice, red wine vinegar, Dijon mustard, oregano, salt, and pepper.
3. **Combine Salad and Vinaigrette:** Pour the vinaigrette over the salad and toss gently to coat.
4. **Add Feta Cheese (Optional):** If using, crumble feta cheese over the salad.
5. **Garnish:** Sprinkle with chopped chives and red pepper flakes (optional) for a final touch.
6. **Serve:** Serve the salad immediately or chill it in the refrigerator for 30 minutes before serving.

Nutritional Information per Serving: Calories: 180, Protein: 4g, Carbohydrates: 6g, Fat: 15g, Fiber: 2g, Cholesterol: 10mg, Sodium: 150mg, Potassium: 400mg

12.4 Tomato & Basil Salad with Olive Oil & Balsamic Glaze
Yields: 4 servings **Prep Time:** 15 minutes **Cook Time:** None

Ingredients:

Salad:

- 2 pounds ripe tomatoes, diced
- 1/2 cup chopped red onion
- 1/4 cup chopped fresh basil
- 1/4 cup crumbled feta cheese (optional)
- 1/4 cup sliced black olives (optional)

Olive Oil & Balsamic Glaze:

- 3 tablespoons extra virgin olive oil
- 1 tablespoon balsamic vinegar
- 1 teaspoon Dijon mustard
- 1/4 teaspoon salt
- 1/4 teaspoon black pepper
- 1/4 teaspoon dried oregano

Instructions:

1. **Prepare the Salad:** In a large bowl, combine diced tomatoes, red onion, chopped basil, feta cheese (optional), and black olives (optional).
2. **Make the Glaze:** In a small bowl, whisk together olive oil, balsamic vinegar, Dijon mustard, salt, pepper, oregano until well combined.
3. **Combine Salad and Glaze:** Pour the glaze over the salad and gently toss to coat.
4. **Serve:** Arrange the salad on individual plates and serve immediately.

Nutritional Information per Serving: Calories: 200, Protein: 5g, Carbohydrates: 10g, Fat: 15g, Fiber: 3g, Cholesterol: 10mg, Sodium: 150mg, Potassium: 450mg

13.4 Roasted Asparagus & Goat Cheese Salad with Honey-Mustard Dressing
Yields: 4 servings **Prep Time:** 10 minutes **Cook Time:** 8-10 minutes

Ingredients:

Salad:

- 1 pound asparagus, trimmed and cut into 2-inch pieces
- 1 tablespoon olive oil
- 1/4 teaspoon salt
- 1/4 teaspoon black pepper
- 1/2 cup crumbled goat cheese
- 1/4 cup chopped walnuts (optional)

Honey-Mustard Dressing:

- 1/4 cup mayonnaise
- 2 tablespoons Dijon mustard
- 1 tablespoon honey
- 1 tablespoon lemon juice
- 1/4 teaspoon salt
- 1/4 teaspoon black pepper

Instructions:

1. **Prepare the Asparagus:** Preheat your air fryer to 400°F (200°C). Toss the asparagus with olive oil, salt, and pepper in a bowl.
2. **Air Fry the Asparagus:** Place the asparagus in a single layer in the air fryer basket. Air fry for 8-10 minutes, shaking the basket halfway through cooking to ensure even browning and crisping.
3. **Make the Dressing:** While the asparagus is cooking, whisk together the mayonnaise, Dijon mustard, honey, lemon juice, salt, and pepper in a small bowl until well combined.
4. **Assemble the Salad:** Once the asparagus is cooked, remove it from the air fryer and transfer to a large bowl. Add the crumbled goat cheese and chopped walnuts (if using). Drizzle with the honey-mustard dressing and gently toss to combine.
5. **Serve:** Arrange the salad on individual plates and serve immediately.

Nutritional Information per Serving: Calories: 350, Protein: 12g, Carbohydrates: 10g, Fat: 25g, Fiber: 5g, Cholesterol: 40mg, Sodium: 300mg, Potassium: 400mg

5. Poultry Recipes

1.5 Easy Keto Chicken Tenders
Yields: 4 servings **Prep time:** 5 minutes **Cook time:** 10-12 minutes

Ingredients:

- 1 pound boneless, skinless chicken breasts, cut into strips (about 12 tenders)
- 1/4 cup mayonnaise
- 1/4 cup grated Parmesan cheese

- 1 teaspoon Italian seasoning
- 1/4 teaspoon salt
- 1/8 teaspoon black pepper
- Optional: 1/4 cup chopped fresh parsley

Instructions:

1. **Prepare the chicken:** Pat the chicken tenders dry with paper towels. In a medium bowl, combine the mayonnaise, Parmesan cheese, Italian seasoning, salt, and pepper. Add the chicken tenders to the bowl and toss to coat.
2. **Air fry:** Preheat your air fryer to 400°F (200°C). Place the chicken tenders in the air fryer basket in a single layer, ensuring they're not overcrowded. Air fry for 10-12 minutes, flipping them halfway through cooking, until they are golden brown and cooked through.
3. **Check for doneness:** The chicken tenders are done when they reach an internal temperature of 165°F (74°C) when measured with a meat thermometer.
4. Serve: Remove the chicken tenders from the air fryer and transfer them to a serving plate. Garnish with chopped fresh parsley (optional).

Nutritional Information per serving: Calories: 250, Protein: 30g, Carbohydrates: 2g, Fats: 12g, Fiber: 1g, Cholesterol: 80mg, Sodium: 300mg, Potassium: 200mg

2.5 Crispy Air Fryer Duck Confit with Orange Glaze
Yields: 2 servings **Prep time:** 15 minutes **Cook time:** 30-35 minutes

Ingredients:

For the Duck Confit:

- 2 duck legs, skin on
- 1 tablespoon olive oil
- 1 teaspoon salt

- 1/2 teaspoon black pepper
- 1/4 teaspoon dried thyme
- 1/4 teaspoon dried rosemary

For the Orange Glaze:

- 1/2 cup orange juice
- 1/4 cup honey
- 1 tablespoon balsamic vinegar

- 1/4 teaspoon ground ginger
- Pinch of red pepper flakes (optional)

Instructions:

1. **Prepare the duck legs:** Pat the duck legs dry with paper towels. In a small bowl, combine the olive oil, salt, pepper, thyme, and rosemary. Rub the mixture all over the duck legs, ensuring the skin is well coated.

2. **Air fry the duck legs:** Preheat your air fryer to 375°F (190°C). Place the duck legs in the air fryer basket, skin side up, ensuring they're not overcrowded. Air fry for 20 minutes, then carefully flip the legs over and air fry for another 10-15 minutes, or until the skin is crispy and the internal temperature reaches 165°F (74°C).
3. **Make the orange glaze:** While the duck legs are air frying, combine the orange juice, honey, balsamic vinegar, ginger, and red pepper flakes (optional) in a small saucepan. Bring to a simmer over medium heat and cook for 5-7 minutes, or until the glaze has thickened slightly.
4. **Glaze the duck:** Remove the duck legs from the air fryer and brush the orange glaze generously over the skin. Return the duck legs to the air fryer basket and air fry for another 2-3 minutes, or until the glaze is slightly caramelized.
5. **Serve:** Remove the duck legs from the air fryer and let them rest for 5-10 minutes before serving. Serve immediately with a side of roasted vegetables, cauliflower mash, or a keto-friendly salad.

Nutritional Information per serving: Calories: 600, Protein: 40g, Carbohydrates: 10g, Fats: 40g, Fiber: 2g, Cholesterol: 150mg, Sodium: 300mg, Potassium: 400mg

3.5 Lemon Herb Keto Chicken Breast
Yields: 2 servings **Prep time:** 5 minutes **Cook time:** 10-12 minutes

Ingredients:

- 2 boneless, skinless chicken breasts (about 6-8 ounces each)
- 1 tablespoon olive oil
- 1 tablespoon lemon juice
- 1 teaspoon dried Italian herbs (or a mix of oregano, thyme, basil)
- 1/4 teaspoon salt
- 1/8 teaspoon black pepper
- Optional: 1 tablespoon chopped fresh parsley

Instructions:

1. **Prepare the chicken:** Pat the chicken breasts dry with paper towels. In a small bowl, whisk together the olive oil, lemon juice, Italian herbs, salt, and pepper.
2. **Marinate:** Pour the marinade over the chicken breasts and ensure they are evenly coated. Let them marinate for at least 15 minutes, or up to an hour for maximum flavor.
3. **Air fry:** Preheat your air fryer to 400°F (200°C). Place the chicken breasts in the air fryer basket, ensuring they're not overcrowded. Air fry for 10-12 minutes, flipping halfway through cooking, until the chicken is cooked through and reaches an internal temperature of 165°F (74°C) when measured with a meat thermometer.
4. **Serve:** Remove the chicken breasts from the air fryer and let them rest for 5 minutes before slicing. Garnish with chopped fresh parsley (optional).

Nutritional Information per serving: Calories: 220, Protein: 30g, Carbohydrates: 1g, Fats: 10g, Fiber: 1g, Cholesterol: 80mg, Sodium: 200mg, Potassium: 300mg

4.5 Air Fryer Turkey Taco Bowls with Cauliflower Rice
Yields: 4 servings **Prep time:** 15 minutes **Cook time:** 12-15 minutes

Ingredients:

For the Turkey:
- 1 pound ground turkey
- 1 tablespoon taco seasoning
- 1/2 teaspoon salt
- 1/4 teaspoon black pepper

For the Cauliflower Rice:
- 1 head of cauliflower, riced (about 3 cups)
- 1 tablespoon olive oil
- 1/2 teaspoon salt
- 1/4 teaspoon black pepper

For the Beans:
- 1 (15-ounce) can black beans, rinsed and drained

For the Toppings:
- Shredded cheddar cheese
- Sliced avocado
- Chopped tomatoes
- Chopped onions
- Sour cream or Greek yogurt (optional)
- Salsa (optional)

Instructions:

1. **Prepare the turkey:** In a medium bowl, combine the ground turkey, taco seasoning, salt, and pepper. Mix well until all ingredients are evenly combined.
2. **Air fry the turkey:** Preheat your air fryer to 400°F (200°C). Place the turkey mixture in the air fryer basket in a single layer, ensuring it's not overcrowded. Air fry for 10-12 minutes, breaking up the turkey with a spoon or spatula halfway through cooking, until the turkey is cooked through and browned.
3. **Make the cauliflower rice:** While the turkey is air frying, prepare the cauliflower rice. In a large skillet or griddle over medium heat, heat the olive oil. Add the cauliflower rice, salt, and pepper. Cook for 5-7 minutes stirring occasionally, until the cauliflower rice is tender and slightly browned.
4. **Assemble the taco bowls:** Divide the cauliflower rice among four bowls. Top with the cooked turkey, black beans, and desired toppings.

Nutritional Information per serving: Calories: 400, Protein: 35g, Carbohydrates: 18g, Fats: 20g, Fiber: 10g, Cholesterol: 80mg, Sodium: 450mg, Potassium: 600mg

5.5 Air Fryer Keto Chicken Fajitas
Yields: 2 servings **Prep time:** 10 minutes **Cook time:** 10-12 minutes

Ingredients:

- 1 pound boneless, skinless chicken breast, cut into thin strips
- 1 red bell pepper, thinly sliced
- 1 green bell pepper, thinly sliced
- 1 tablespoon olive oil
- 1 teaspoon fajita seasoning
- 1/4 teaspoon salt
- 1/8 teaspoon black pepper
- Optional: 1/4 cup chopped red onion
- Optional: 1/4 cup chopped cilantro

Instructions:

1. **Prepare the chicken and veggies:** In a large bowl, toss the chicken strips with olive oil, fajita seasoning, salt, and pepper. Set aside. In a separate bowl, toss the sliced bell peppers and red onion (optional) with a little olive oil, salt, and pepper.
2. **Air fry the chicken:** Preheat your air fryer to 400°F (200°C). Place the chicken strips in the air fryer basket in a single layer, ensuring they're not overcrowded. Air fry for 5-7 minutes, flipping halfway through cooking, until they are browned and cooked through.
3. **Air fry the veggies:** Add the sliced bell peppers and red onion (optional) to the air fryer basket. Air fry for 3-5 minutes, until tender and slightly charred.
4. **Serve:** Remove the cooked chicken and veggies from the air fryer. Serve immediately, garnished with chopped cilantro (optional).

Nutritional Information per serving: Calories: 350, Protein: 30g, Carbohydrates: 10g, Fats: 18g, Fiber: 4g, Cholesterol: 90mg, Sodium: 350mg, Potassium: 500mg

6.5 Spicy Keto Chicken Drumsticks
Yields: 4 servings **Prep time:** 5 minutes **Cook time:** 20-25 minutes

Ingredients:

- 8 chicken drumsticks
- 2 tablespoons olive oil
- 1 tablespoon paprika
- 1 teaspoon chili powder
- 1/2 teaspoon garlic powder

- 1/4 teaspoon onion powder
- 1/4 teaspoon salt
- 1/8 teaspoon black pepper
- Optional: 1/2 teaspoon cayenne pepper (for extra heat)

Instructions:

1. **Prepare the chicken:** Pat the chicken drumsticks dry with paper towels. In a medium bowl, combine the olive oil, paprika, chili powder, garlic powder, onion powder, salt, pepper, and cayenne pepper (optional). Toss the chicken drumsticks in the mixture, ensuring they are evenly coated.
2. **Air fry:** Preheat your air fryer to 400°F (200°C). Place the chicken drumsticks in the air fryer basket in a single layer, ensuring they're not overcrowded. Air fry for 20-25 minutes, flipping them halfway through cooking, until they are golden brown and cooked through. The internal temperature should reach 165°F (74°C) when measured with a meat thermometer.
3. **Serve:** Remove the chicken drumsticks from the air fryer and let them rest for 5 minutes before serving.

Nutritional Information per serving: Calories: 280, Protein: 25g, Carbohydrates: 0g, Fats: 18g, Fiber: 0g, Cholesterol: 100mg, Sodium: 250mg, Potassium: 200mg

7.5 Air Fryer Turkey Pot Pie with Creamy Mushroom Sauce
Yields: 2 servings **Prep time:** 15 minutes **Cook time:** 15-20 minutes

Ingredients:

For the Turkey Filling:

- 1 pound ground turkey
- 1 tablespoon olive oil
- 1 onion, chopped
- 2 cloves garlic, minced
- 1 (10.75 ounce) can condensed cream of mushroom soup

- 1/2 cup chicken broth
- 1/2 teaspoon dried thyme
- 1/4 teaspoon salt
- 1/8 teaspoon black pepper

For the Mushroom Sauce:

- 1 tablespoon olive oil
- 1 cup sliced mushrooms (cremini, button, or shiitake)
- 1/4 cup heavy cream

- 1/4 cup grated Parmesan cheese
- 1 teaspoon garlic powder
- 1/4 teaspoon salt
- 1/8 teaspoon black pepper

For the Crust:

- 1 cup almond flour
- 1/4 cup grated Parmesan cheese
- 1/4 teaspoon garlic powder

- 1/4 teaspoon salt
- 1/4 cup melted butter
- 1 egg, beaten

Instructions:

1. **Prepare the turkey filling:** In a large skillet over medium heat, heat the olive oil. Add the chopped onion and cook until softened, about 5 minutes. Stir in the minced garlic and cook for another minute. Add the ground turkey and cook until browned, breaking up the turkey with a spoon or spatula. Drain any excess fat.
2. **Combine the filling ingredients:** Add the cream of mushroom soup, chicken broth, thyme, salt, and pepper to the skillet. Stir to combine and bring to a simmer.
3. **Make the mushroom sauce:** While the turkey filling is simmering, heat the olive oil in a small saucepan over medium heat. Add the sliced mushrooms and cook until softened and browned, about 5-7 minutes. Stir in the heavy cream, Parmesan cheese, garlic powder, salt, and pepper. Simmer for 2-3 minutes, or until the sauce has thickened slightly.
4. **Prepare the crust:** Preheat your air fryer to 400°F (200°C). In a medium bowl, combine the almond flour, Parmesan cheese, garlic powder, and salt. Stir in the melted butter until a dough forms. Knead the dough for few seconds until it is smooth.
5. **Assemble the pot pie:** Divide the turkey filling evenly between two ramekins or small oven-safe dishes. T with the mushroom sauce. Divide the dough in half and roll each half into a circle large enough to cover the top of the ramekins. Gently press the dough onto the top of the filling, crimping the edges to seal. Brush the top of the crust with the beaten egg.
6. **Air fry the pot pie:** Place the ramekins in the air fryer basket, ensuring they're not overcrowded. Air fry fc 10-12 minutes, or until the crust is golden brown and the filling is bubbly.

Nutritional Information per serving: Calories: 400, Protein: 30g, Carbohydrates: 12g, Fats: 25g, Fiber: 4g, Cholesterol: 100mg, Sodium: 450mg, Potassium: 500mg

8.5 Garlic Parmesan Keto Chicken Cutlets
Yields: 2 servings **Prep time:** 10 minutes **Cook time:** 10-12 minutes

Ingredients:

- 1 pound boneless, skinless chicken breasts, sliced into thin cutlets
- 1/2 cup grated Parmesan cheese
- 1/4 cup almond flour
- 1 teaspoon garlic powder

- 1/2 teaspoon Italian seasoning
- 1/4 teaspoon salt
- 1/8 teaspoon black pepper
- 1 tablespoon olive oil

Instructions:

1. **Prepare the chicken:** In a shallow bowl, combine the Parmesan cheese, almond flour, garlic powder, Italian seasoning, salt, and pepper.
2. **Coat the chicken:** Dip each chicken cutlet into the cheese mixture, ensuring they are evenly coated.
3. **Air fry:** Preheat your air fryer to 400°F (200°C). Place the coated chicken cutlets in the air fryer basket in a single layer, ensuring they're not overcrowded. Air fry for 10-12 minutes, flipping them halfway through cooking, until they are cooked through and the breading is golden brown.
4. **Serve:** Remove the chicken cutlets from the air fryer and let them rest for 2-3 minutes before serving.

Nutritional Information per serving: Calories: 350, Protein: 35g, Carbohydrates: 5g, Fats: 20g, Fiber: 2g, Cholesterol: 100mg, Sodium: 400mg, Potassium: 300mg

9.5 Easy Air Fryer Duck Breast with Cherry Sauce
Yields: 2 servings **Prep time:** 10 minutes **Cook time:** 15-20 minutes

Ingredients:

For the Duck Breast:

- 2 boneless, skin-on duck breasts
- 1 tablespoon olive oil
- 1 teaspoon salt

- 1/2 teaspoon black pepper
- 1/4 teaspoon dried thyme

For the Cherry Sauce:

- 1 cup pitted cherries (fresh or frozen)
- 1/4 cup red wine vinegar
- 1 tablespoon honey

- 1/4 teaspoon ground ginger
- Pinch of red pepper flakes (optional)

Instructions:

1. **Prepare the duck breasts:** Pat the duck breasts dry with paper towels. Score the skin with a sharp knife, creating a criss-cross pattern. This will help the skin to render more evenly and become crispy.
2. **Season the duck breasts:** In a small bowl, combine the olive oil, salt, pepper, and thyme. Rub the mixture all over the duck breasts, ensuring the skin is well coated.
3. **Air fry the duck breasts:** Preheat your air fryer to 400°F (200°C). Place the duck breasts in the air fryer basket, skin side up, ensuring they're not overcrowded. Air fry for 10-12 minutes, or until the skin is crispy and the internal temperature reaches 135°F (57°C) for medium-rare.

4. **Make the cherry sauce:** While the duck breasts are air frying, combine the cherries, red wine vinegar, honey, ginger, and red pepper flakes (optional) in a small saucepan. Bring to a simmer over medium heat and cook for 5-7 minutes, or until the sauce has thickened slightly.
5. **Rest and serve:** Remove the duck breasts from the air fryer and let them rest for 5-10 minutes before slicing. Serve the duck breast with the cherry sauce drizzled over top. Enjoy with a side of roasted vegetables, cauliflower mash, or a keto-friendly salad.

Nutritional Information per serving: Calories: 500, Protein: 35g, Carbohydrates: 10g, Fats: 30g, Fiber: 2g, Cholesterol: 150mg, Sodium: 300mg, Potassium: 400mg

10.5 Keto Chicken Parmesan with Low-Carb Breadcrumbs
Yields: 2 servings Prep time: 10 minutes Cook time: 15-20 minutes

Ingredients:

- 2 boneless, skinless chicken breasts (about 6-8 ounces each)
- 1/4 cup grated Parmesan cheese
- 1/4 cup almond flour
- 1/4 cup finely grated Pecorino Romano cheese
- 1/2 teaspoon dried oregano
- 1/4 teaspoon salt
- 1/8 teaspoon black pepper
- 1/4 cup marinara sauce
- 2 tablespoons mozzarella cheese, shredded

Instructions:

1. **Prepare the chicken:** Pat the chicken breasts dry with paper towels. In a small bowl, combine the Parmesan cheese, almond flour, Pecorino Romano cheese, oregano, salt, and pepper.
2. **Coat the chicken:** Dip the chicken breasts in the cheese mixture, ensuring they are evenly coated.
3. **Air fry:** Preheat your air fryer to 400°F (200°C). Place the coated chicken breasts in the air fryer basket in a single layer, ensuring they're not overcrowded. Air fry for 10-12 minutes, flipping halfway through cooking, until the chicken is cooked through and the breadcrumb coating is golden brown.
4. **Top with sauce and cheese:** Remove the chicken from the air fryer and place it on a serving plate. Top each chicken breast with 2 tablespoons of marinara sauce and 1 tablespoon of mozzarella cheese.
5. **Broil (optional):** Place the chicken under the broiler for 1-2 minutes, or until the mozzarella cheese is melted and bubbly.
6. **Serve:** Serve immediately with a side of your favorite keto-friendly vegetables or a low-carb pasta alternative.

Nutritional Information per serving: Calories: 400, Protein: 35g, Carbohydrates: 10g, Fats: 20g, Fiber: 2g, Cholesterol: 100mg, Sodium: 400mg, Potassium: 300mg

11.5 Air Fryer Keto Chicken Tikka Masala
Yields: 2 servings Prep time: 15 minutes Cook time: 30 minutes

Ingredients:

- **For the Chicken:**
  - 1 pound boneless, skinless chicken breast, cut into 1-inch cubes
  - 1/2 teaspoon ground cumin
  - 1/2 teaspoon turmeric

- o 1 tablespoon olive oil
- o 1 teaspoon garam masala
- **For the Tikka Masala Sauce:**
  - o 1 tablespoon olive oil
  - o 1 olive oil, finely chopped
  - o 2 cloves garlic, minced
  - o 1 (14-ounce) can diced tomatoes, undrained
  - o 1/2 cup heavy cream
  - o 1 tablespoon tomato paste
  - o 1 teaspoon garam masala

- o 1/4 teaspoon salt
- o 1/8 teaspoon black pepper

- o 1/2 teaspoon ground cumin
- o 1/4 teaspoon red pepper flakes (optional)
- o 1/4 teaspoon salt
- o 1/8 teaspoon black pepper
- o Optional: 1/4 cup chopped cilantro for garnish

Instructions:

1. **Prepare the chicken:** In a medium bowl, combine the chicken cubes, olive oil, garam masala, cumin, turmeric, salt, and pepper. Toss to coat the chicken evenly.
2. **Air fry the chicken:** Preheat your air fryer to 400°F (200°C). Place the marinated chicken cubes in the air fryer basket in a single layer, ensuring they're not overcrowded. Air fry for 8-10 minutes, shaking the basket halfway through cooking, until the chicken is cooked through and slightly browned.
3. **Make the Tikka Masala sauce:** While the chicken is air frying, heat the olive oil in a medium saucepan over medium heat. Add the chopped onion and cook until softened, about 5 minutes. Stir in the minced garlic and cook for another minute.
4. **Combine the ingredients:** Add the diced tomatoes, heavy cream, tomato paste, garam masala, cumin, red pepper flakes (optional), salt, and pepper to the saucepan. Bring to a simmer and cook for 10-15 minutes, or until the sauce has thickened slightly.
5. **Combine and serve:** Add the cooked chicken to the sauce and stir to coat. Serve immediately, garnished with chopped cilantro (optional).

Nutritional Information per serving: Calories: 450, Protein: 35g, Carbohydrates: 10g, Fats: 25g, Fiber: 4g, Cholesterol: 100mg, Sodium: 400mg, Potassium: 500mg

12.5 Air Fryer Turkey Meatballs with Spicy Marinara Sauce
Yields: 4 servings **Prep time:** 15 minutes **Cook time:** 12-15 minutes

Ingredients:

For the Turkey Meatballs:

- 1 pound ground turkey
- 1/2 cup almond flour
- 1/4 cup grated Parmesan cheese
- 1 egg
- 1/4 cup finely chopped onion

- 1 clove garlic, minced
- 1 teaspoon Italian seasoning
- 1/2 teaspoon salt
- 1/4 teaspoon black pepper

For the Spicy Marinara Sauce:

- 1 (15-ounce) can crushed tomatoes
- 1/4 cup tomato paste
- 1/2 teaspoon dried oregano
- 1/4 teaspoon dried basil

- 1/8 teaspoon onion powder
- 1/4 teaspoon red pepper flakes (adjust to taste for desired spiciness)

- 1/4 teaspoon garlic powder
- Salt and pepper to taste

Instructions:

1. **Prepare the meatballs:** In a large bowl, combine the ground turkey, almond flour, Parmesan cheese, egg, onion, garlic, Italian seasoning, salt, and pepper. Mix well until all ingredients are evenly combined.
2. **Form the meatballs:** Roll the meat mixture into 12-15 meatballs.
3. **Air fry the meatballs:** Preheat your air fryer to 400°F (200°C). Place the meatballs in the air fryer basket in single layer, ensuring they're not overcrowded. Air fry for 12-15 minutes, shaking the basket halfway throug cooking, until the meatballs are cooked through and golden brown.
4. **Make the spicy marinara sauce:** While the meatballs are air frying, prepare the marinara sauce. In a medium saucepan, combine the crushed tomatoes, tomato paste, oregano, basil, garlic powder, onion powde red pepper flakes, salt, and pepper. Bring to a simmer over medium heat and cook for 10-15 minutes, or unt the sauce has thickened.
5. **Combine and serve:** Once the meatballs and the sauce are ready, add the meatballs to the marinara sauce a stir to coat. Simmer for a few minutes to allow the flavors to blend. Serve immediately with a side of your favorite keto-friendly accompaniments.

Nutritional Information per serving: Calories: 300, Protein: 30g, Carbohydrates: 5g, Fats: 20g, Fiber: 2g, Cholesterol: 80mg, Sodium: 400mg, Potassium: 300mg

13.5 Creamy Keto Chicken Alfredo with Zucchini Noodles
Yields: 2 servings **Prep time:** 10 minutes **Cook time:** 15-20 minutes

Ingredients:

For the Chicken:

- 1 pound boneless, skinless chicken breast, cut into bite-sized pieces
- 1 tablespoon olive oil
- 1 teaspoon Italian seasoning
- 1/2 teaspoon salt
- 1/4 teaspoon black pepper

For the Creamy Alfredo Sauce:

- 1 cup heavy cream
- 1/2 cup grated Parmesan cheese
- 1/4 cup cream cheese, softened
- 1/4 teaspoon garlic powder
- 1/8 teaspoon onion powder
- Salt and pepper to taste

For the Zucchini Noodles:

- 1 medium zucchini, spiralized into noodles
- 1 tablespoon olive oil
- 1/4 teaspoon salt

Instructions:

1. **Prepare the chicken:** In a medium bowl, combine the chicken pieces, olive oil, Italian seasoning, salt, an pepper. Toss to coat evenly.

2. **Air fry the chicken:** Preheat your air fryer to 400°F (200°C). Place the chicken in the air fryer basket in a single layer, ensuring they're not overcrowded. Air fry for 10-12 minutes, shaking the basket halfway through cooking, until the chicken is cooked through and golden brown.
3. **Make the creamy alfredo sauce:** While the chicken is air frying, prepare the alfredo sauce. In a small saucepan over medium heat, combine the heavy cream, Parmesan cheese, cream cheese, garlic powder, onion powder, salt, and pepper. Bring to a simmer and cook for 5-7 minutes, or until the sauce has thickened.
4. **Cook the zucchini noodles:** In a large skillet or griddle over medium heat, heat the olive oil. Add the zucchini noodles and salt and cook for 3-4 minutes, or until the noodles are tender-crisp.
5. **Combine and serve:** Add the cooked chicken and creamy alfredo sauce to the zucchini noodles and stir to combine. Cook for an additional 2-3 minutes, or until the sauce is heated through. Taste and adjust seasonings as needed. Serve immediately, garnished with additional Parmesan cheese (optional).

Nutritional Information per serving: Calories: 400, Protein: 30g, Carbohydrates: 10g, Fats: 25g, Fiber: 5g, Cholesterol: 100mg, Sodium: 400mg, Potassium: 500mg

14.5 Keto Turkey Chili with Black Beans & Avocado
Yields: 4 servings **Prep time:** 15 minutes **Cook time:** 15-20 minutes

Ingredients:

- 1 pound ground turkey
- 1 (15-ounce) can black beans, rinsed and drained
- 1 (15-ounce) can diced tomatoes, undrained
- 1 (10.75-ounce) can diced green chilies, undrained
- 1 onion, chopped
- 2 cloves garlic, minced
- 1 tablespoon chili powder
- 1 teaspoon cumin

- 1/2 teaspoon oregano
- 1/4 teaspoon cayenne pepper (optional, for extra heat)
- 1/2 teaspoon salt
- 1/4 teaspoon black pepper
- 1 avocado, diced
- Optional: 1/4 cup chopped cilantro for garnish
- Optional: 1 tablespoon sour cream or Greek yogurt for garnish

Instructions:

1. **Prepare the turkey:** In a medium bowl, combine the ground turkey, chili powder, cumin, oregano, cayenne pepper (optional), salt, and pepper. Mix well until all ingredients are evenly combined.
2. **Air fry the turkey:** Preheat your air fryer to 400°F (200°C). Place the turkey mixture in the air fryer basket in a single layer, ensuring it's not overcrowded. Air fry for 10-12 minutes, breaking up the turkey with a spoon or spatula halfway through cooking, until the turkey is cooked through and browned.
3. **Make the chili:** While the turkey is air frying, prepare the chili. In a large pot or Dutch oven, combine the diced tomatoes, green chilies, onion, and garlic. Bring to a simmer over medium heat and cook for 5-7 minutes, or until the onions are softened.
4. **Combine and cook:** Add the cooked turkey to the pot with the tomato mixture. Stir in the black beans. Bring to a simmer and cook for an additional 5-7 minutes, or until the chili has thickened slightly. Taste and adjust seasonings as needed.
5. **Serve:** Ladle the chili into bowls and top with diced avocado, chopped cilantro (optional), and a dollop of sour cream or Greek yogurt (optional).

Nutritional Information per serving: Calories: 350, Protein: 30g, Carbohydrates: 15g, Fats: 15g, Fiber: 10g, Cholesterol: 80mg, Sodium: 400mg, Potassium: 500mg

15.5 Keto Chicken Curry with Coconut Milk

Yields: 2 servings **Prep time:** 15 minutes **Cook time:** 15-20 minutes

Ingredients:

- **For the Chicken:**

  - 1 pound boneless, skinless chicken breast, cut into 1-inch cubes
  - 1 tablespoon olive oil
  - 1 teaspoon curry powder
  - 1/2 teaspoon ground cumin
  - 1/4 teaspoon turmeric
  - 1/4 teaspoon salt
  - 1/8 teaspoon black pepper

- **For the Curry Sauce:**

  - 1 tablespoon olive oil
  - 1 onion, finely chopped
  - 2 cloves garlic, minced
  - 1 (14-ounce) can full-fat coconut milk
  - 1/4 cup heavy cream (optional, for extra richness)
  - 1 teaspoon curry powder
  - 1/2 teaspoon ground cumin
  - 1/4 teaspoon turmeric
  - 1/4 teaspoon salt
  - 1/8 teaspoon black pepper
  - Optional: 1/4 cup chopped cilantro for garnish
  - Optional: 1/4 teaspoon red pepper flakes for a spicy kick

Instructions:

1. **Prepare the chicken:** In a medium bowl, combine the chicken cubes, olive oil, curry powder, cumin, turmeric, salt, and pepper. Toss to coat the chicken evenly.
2. **Air fry the chicken:** Preheat your air fryer to 400°F (200°C). Place the marinated chicken cubes in the air fryer basket in a single layer, ensuring they're not overcrowded. Air fry for 8-10 minutes, shaking the basket halfway through cooking, until the chicken is cooked through and slightly browned.
3. **Make the curry sauce:** While the chicken is air frying, heat the olive oil in a medium saucepan over medium heat. Add the chopped onion and cook until softened, about 5 minutes. Stir in the minced garlic and cook for another minute.
4. **Combine the ingredients:** Add the coconut milk, heavy cream (optional), curry powder, cumin, turmeric, salt, and pepper to the saucepan. Bring to a simmer and cook for 10-15 minutes, or until the sauce has thickened slightly.
5. **Combine and serve:** Add the cooked chicken to the sauce and stir to coat. Simmer for another 2-3 minutes allow the flavors to blend. Serve immediately, garnished with chopped cilantro and red pepper flakes (optional).

Nutritional Information per serving: Calories: 450, Protein: 35g, Carbohydrates: 10g, Fats: 25g, Fiber: 4g, Cholesterol: 100mg, Sodium: 400mg, Potassium: 500mg

1.6 Juicy Keto Air Fryer Steak with Garlic Herb Butter
Yield: 1 serving **Prep time:** 5 minutes **Cook time:** 10-15 minutes

Ingredients:

- 1 (6-8 oz) ribeye, New York strip, or sirloin steak
- 1 tbsp olive oil
- 1 tbsp unsalted butter
- 2 cloves garlic, minced

- 1 tsp dried oregano
- 1/2 tsp dried thyme
- Salt and black pepper to taste
- 1 tbsp chopped fresh parsley (optional)

Instructions:

1. **Prepare the steak:** Pat the steak dry with paper towels. Season generously with salt and pepper.
2. **Preheat the air fryer:** Preheat your air fryer to 400°F (200°C).
3. **Cook the steak:** Place the steak in the air fryer basket. Cook for 5-7 minutes per side for medium-rare, adjusting the time based on your desired level of doneness.
4. **Make the garlic herb butter:** While the steak cooks, melt the butter in a small saucepan over medium heat. Add the minced garlic, oregano, and thyme. Stir until fragrant, about 1 minute.
5. **Rest and serve:** Remove the steak from the air fryer and let it rest for 5 minutes before slicing. Spoon the garlic herb butter over the steak and garnish with chopped parsley, if desired.

Nutritional Information (per serving): Calories: 500, Protein: 40g, Carbohydrates: 2g, Fat: 35g, Fiber: 1g, Cholesterol: 120mg, Sodium: 200mg, Potassium: 300mg

2.6 Crispy Keto Ground Beef Tacos
Yield: 4 servings **Prep time:** 5 minutes **Cook time:** 10 minutes

Ingredients:

- 1 lb ground beef
- 1 tbsp olive oil
- 1/2 tsp chili powder
- 1/4 tsp cumin
- 1/4 tsp paprika
- 1/4 tsp garlic powder

- Salt and pepper to taste
- 4 lettuce leaves (or your favorite low-carb tortillas)
- Toppings (optional): shredded cheese, diced avocado, chopped cilantro, salsa, sour cream

Instructions:

1. **Preheat the air fryer:** Preheat your air fryer to 400°F (200°C).
2. **Prepare the ground beef:** In a bowl, combine the ground beef, olive oil, chili powder, cumin, paprika, garlic powder, salt, and pepper. Mix well.
3. **Cook the ground beef:** Place the ground beef mixture in the air fryer basket, spreading it out in an even layer. Cook for 8-10 minutes, shaking the basket halfway through, until the beef is cooked through and crispy.
4. **Assemble the tacos:** Once the beef is cooked, transfer it to a bowl. Warm your lettuce leaves (or tortillas) in the air fryer for a few minutes, if desired.
5. **Fill and top:** Spoon the crispy ground beef mixture into your lettuce leaves (or tortillas) and top with your favorite keto-friendly toppings.

Nutritional Information (per serving): Calories: 400, Protein: 30g, Carbohydrates: 5g, Fat: 25g, Fiber: 2g, Cholesterol: 100mg, Sodium: 250mg, Potassium: 300mg

3.6 Easy Keto Meatballs with Marinara Sauce
Yield: 4 servings **Prep time:** 10 minutes **Cook time:** 15 minutes

Ingredients:

- 1 lb ground beef
- 1/2 cup grated Parmesan cheese
- 1 egg
- 1/4 cup chopped onion
- 2 cloves garlic, minced
- 1 tbsp dried oregano
- 1/2 tsp dried basil
- Salt and pepper to taste
- 1 cup marinara sauce (store-bought or homemade)
- 1 tbsp olive oil (for the sauce)
- Optional toppings: chopped fresh parsley, shredded mozzarella

Instructions:

1. **Preheat the air fryer:** Preheat your air fryer to 400°F (200°C).
2. **Prepare the meatballs:** In a large bowl, combine the ground beef, Parmesan cheese, egg, onion, garlic, oregano, basil, salt, and pepper. Mix well until just combined.
3. **Form the meatballs:** Using your hands, shape the mixture into 1-inch meatballs.
4. **Air fry the meatballs:** Place the meatballs in the air fryer basket, making sure they aren't touching. Air fry for 10-12 minutes, shaking the basket halfway through, until cooked through and browned.
5. **Prepare the sauce:** While the meatballs cook, heat the olive oil in a small saucepan over medium heat. Add the marinara sauce and simmer for 5-7 minutes, stirring occasionally.
6. **Serve:** Once the meatballs are cooked, serve them with the marinara sauce. Garnish with chopped parsley and shredded mozzarella, if desired.

Nutritional Information (per serving): Calories: 450, Protein: 30g, Carbohydrates: 10g, Fat: 25g, Fiber: 3g, Cholesterol: 100mg, Sodium: 300mg, Potassium: 400mg

4.6 Spicy Keto Chili with Ground Beef
Yield: 4 servings **Prep time:** 10 minutes **Cook time:** 20 minutes

Ingredients:

- 1 lb ground beef
- 1 tbsp olive oil
- 1 onion, chopped
- 2 cloves garlic, minced
- 1 (15 oz) can diced tomatoes, undrained
- 1 (15 oz) can kidney beans, drained and rinsed (optional, for added protein and fiber)
- 1 (10 oz) can diced green chilies, undrained
- 1 tbsp chili powder
- 1 tsp cumin
- 1/2 tsp smoked paprika
- 1/4 tsp cayenne pepper (adjust to your spice preference)
- Salt and black pepper to taste
- Optional toppings: shredded cheese, sour cream, avocado, cilantro, jalapeños

Instructions:

1. **Preheat the air fryer:** Preheat your air fryer to 400°F (200°C).
2. **Cook the ground beef:** In a large bowl, combine the ground beef and olive oil. Mix well and then spread in an even layer in the air fryer basket. Cook for 8-10 minutes, shaking the basket halfway through, until browned and cooked through.
3. **Sauté the onions and garlic:** While the beef cooks, heat a large skillet over medium heat. Add the chopped onion and cook until softened, about 5 minutes. Add the minced garlic and cook for another minute.
4. **Combine ingredients:** Transfer the cooked beef to the skillet with the onion and garlic mixture. Add the diced tomatoes, kidney beans (if using), green chilies, chili powder, cumin, paprika, cayenne pepper, salt, and pepper. Bring to a simmer and cook for 10 minutes, stirring occasionally, to allow the flavors to meld.
5. **Serve:** Spoon the chili into bowls and top with your favorite keto-friendly toppings.

Nutritional Information (per serving): Calories: 450, Protein: 30g, Carbohydrates: 20g, Fat: 20g, Fiber: 8g, Cholesterol: 90mg, Sodium: 500mg, Potassium: 500mg

5.6 Air Fryer Keto Beef & Broccoli Stir-Fry
Yield: 2 servings **Prep time:** 10 minutes **Cook time:** 12 minutes

Ingredients:

- 1/2 lb sirloin steak, thinly sliced
- 1 tbsp olive oil
- 1 head broccoli, cut into florets
- 1/4 cup soy sauce
- 1 tbsp rice vinegar
- 1 tbsp sesame oil
- 1 clove garlic, minced
- 1 tsp ginger, grated
- 1/2 tsp black pepper
- 1/4 tsp red pepper flakes (optional, for added spice)
- 1 tbsp chopped green onions (for garnish)
- 1 tbsp sesame seeds (for garnish)

Instructions:

1. **Prepare the ingredients:** Cut the sirloin steak into thin strips. Wash and cut the broccoli into bite-sized florets.
2. **Marinade the beef:** In a bowl, combine the soy sauce, rice vinegar, sesame oil, minced garlic, grated ginger, black pepper, and red pepper flakes (if using). Add the sliced beef and toss to coat. Marinate for at least 15 minutes.
3. **Preheat the air fryer:** Preheat your air fryer to 400°F (200°C).
4. **Air fry the beef:** Place the marinated beef in the air fryer basket, spreading it out in an even layer. Cook for 4-5 minutes, shaking the basket halfway through, until browned.
5. **Air fry the broccoli:** Add the broccoli florets to the air fryer basket with the cooked beef. Drizzle with 1 tablespoon of olive oil and toss gently. Air fry for another 6-7 minutes, shaking the basket halfway through, until the broccoli is tender-crisp.
6. **Assemble and serve:** Once the beef and broccoli are cooked, toss them together in the air fryer basket. Serve immediately, garnished with chopped green onions and sesame seeds.

Nutritional Information (per serving): Calories: 400, Protein: 30g, Carbohydrates: 10g, Fat: 20g, Fiber: 5g, Cholesterol: 80mg, Sodium: 500mg, Potassium: 400mg

6.6 Flavorful Keto Beef Brisket
Yield: 4-6 servings **Prep time:** 15 minutes **Cook time:** 45-60 minutes

Ingredients:

- 2-3 lb beef brisket, trimmed of excess fat
- 2 tbsp olive oil
- 1 tbsp smoked paprika
- 1 tsp garlic powder
- 1 tsp onion powder
- 1/2 tsp black pepper

- 1/4 tsp cayenne pepper (optional, for added spice)
- 1/2 cup beef broth (or water)
- 1/4 cup apple cider vinegar
- 1 tbsp Worcestershire sauce
- 1 tbsp brown sugar (optional, for added sweetness)
- Salt to taste

Instructions:

1. **Prepare the brisket:** Pat the beef brisket dry with paper towels. Cut it into 2-3 inch pieces.
2. **Marinate the brisket:** In a bowl, combine the olive oil, smoked paprika, garlic powder, onion powder, black pepper, and cayenne pepper (if using). Mix well and add the brisket pieces, tossing to coat evenly. Let the brisket marinate for at least 30 minutes, or up to 2 hours.
3. **Preheat the air fryer:** Preheat your air fryer to 350°F (175°C).
4. **Cook the brisket:** Place the marinated brisket pieces in the air fryer basket, ensuring they are not overcrowded. Cook for 20 minutes, then flip the pieces over and continue cooking for another 20 minutes.
5. **Add the sauce:** While the brisket is cooking, combine the beef broth, apple cider vinegar, Worcestershire sauce, and brown sugar (if using) in a small saucepan. Heat over medium heat until the sugar dissolves and the sauce is slightly thickened.
6. **Finish cooking:** After the initial 40 minutes of cooking, pour the sauce over the brisket pieces in the air fryer. Continue cooking for another 15-20 minutes, shaking the basket halfway through, until the brisket is fork-tender and the sauce has reduced and thickened.
7. **Rest and serve:** Once cooked, remove the brisket from the air fryer and let it rest for 5-10 minutes before serving.

Nutritional Information (per serving): Calories: 400, Protein: 30g, Carbohydrates: 5g, Fat: 25g, Fiber: 2g, Cholesterol: 100mg, Sodium: 400mg, Potassium: 300mg

7.6 Cheesy Keto Beef & Spinach Dip
Yield: 4 servings **Prep time:** 10 minutes **Cook time:** 10-12 minutes

Ingredients:

- 1 lb ground beef
- 1 tbsp olive oil
- 1/2 onion, chopped
- 2 cloves garlic, minced
- 1 (10 oz) package frozen chopped spinach, thawed and squeezed dry
- 1 cup shredded cheddar cheese
- 1/2 cup cream cheese, softened

- 1/4 cup sour cream
- 1/4 cup grated Parmesan cheese
- 1/4 tsp garlic powder
- 1/4 tsp onion powder
- Salt and pepper to taste
- Optional toppings: chopped green onions, sliced black olives

Instructions:

1. **Preheat the air fryer:** Preheat your air fryer to 350°F (175°C).
2. **Cook the beef:** In a large skillet over medium heat, cook the ground beef with the olive oil until browned and cooked through. Drain any excess grease.
3. **Sauté the onions and garlic:** Add the chopped onion and minced garlic to the skillet and cook until softened, about 5 minutes.
4. **Combine ingredients:** Stir in the thawed and squeezed spinach, cheddar cheese, cream cheese, sour cream, Parmesan cheese, garlic powder, onion powder, salt, and pepper. Mix well until everything is combined.
5. **Air fry the dip:** Transfer the mixture to an oven-safe dish or ramekin that fits in your air fryer. Air fry for 8-10 minutes, or until the dip is heated through and bubbly.
6. **Serve:** Remove the dip from the air fryer and let it cool slightly before serving. Garnish with your favorite toppings, if desired.

Nutritional Information (per serving): Calories: 450, Protein: 25g, Carbohydrates: 10g, Fat: 30g, Fiber: 3g, Cholesterol: 100mg, Sodium: 400mg, Potassium: 300mg

8.6 Air Fryer Keto Beef Empanadas
Yield: 6 servings **Prep time:** 20 minutes **Cook time:** 12-15 minutes

Ingredients:

For the Dough:

*   1 cup almond flour
*   1/4 cup grated Parmesan cheese
*   1/4 cup melted butter, cooled slightly
*   1 large egg, beaten
*   1/4 tsp salt
*   1/4 tsp garlic powder

For the Filling:

*   1 lb ground beef
*   1 tbsp olive oil
*   1/2 onion, chopped
*   2 cloves garlic, minced
*   1 (15 oz) can diced tomatoes, undrained
*   1 (4 oz) can diced green chilies, undrained
*   1 tsp chili powder
*   1/2 tsp cumin
*   1/4 tsp cayenne pepper (optional, for added spice)
*   Salt and pepper to taste
*   1/2 cup shredded cheddar cheese

Instructions:

1. **Prepare the dough:** In a large bowl, combine the almond flour, Parmesan cheese, melted butter, beaten egg, salt, and garlic powder. Mix well until a dough forms. If the dough is too dry, add a tablespoon of water at a time until it comes together.
2. **Prepare the filling:** In a large skillet over medium heat, cook the ground beef with the olive oil until browned and cooked through. Drain any excess grease. Add the onion and garlic and cook until softened, about 5 minutes. Stir in the diced tomatoes, green chilies, chili powder, cumin, cayenne pepper (if using), salt, and pepper. Simmer for 5 minutes to allow the flavors to meld.
3. **Assemble the empanadas:** Divide the dough into 6 equal portions. Roll out each portion into a 6-inch circle. Spoon about 1/4 cup of the filling onto the center of each circle. Top with a tablespoon of shredded cheddar cheese. Fold the dough over to form a half-circle and pinch the edges to seal.
4. **Preheat the air fryer:** Preheat your air fryer to 375°F (190°C).

5. **Air fry the empanadas:** Place the empanadas in the air fryer basket, ensuring they are not touching. Air fry for 8-10 minutes, or until the crust is golden brown and crispy. Flip the empanadas halfway through cooking for even browning.
6. **Serve:** Remove the empanadas from the air fryer and let them cool slightly before serving.

Nutritional Information (per serving): Calories: 400, Protein: 25g, Carbohydrates: 10g, Fat: 25g, Fiber: 3g, Cholesterol: 100mg, Sodium: 300mg, Potassium: 300mg

9.6 Keto Beef Stroganoff with Cauliflower Rice
Yields: 4 Servings **Prep Time:** 15 minutes **Cook Time:** 20 minutes

Ingredients:

- 1 lb. lean ground beef
- 1 onion, finely chopped
- 2 cloves garlic, minced
- 1 (10.75 oz) can condensed cream of mushroom soup (undiluted)
- 1/2 cup heavy cream
- 1/4 cup sour cream
- 1 tablespoon Dijon mustard
- 1/2 teaspoon dried thyme

- 1/4 teaspoon salt
- 1/4 teaspoon black pepper
- 1 head cauliflower, cut into rice-sized florets
- 2 tablespoons butter (optional, for added richness)
- 1/4 cup chopped fresh parsley (for garnish, optional)

Instructions:

1. **Prepare Cauliflower Rice:** Preheat the air fryer to 400°F (200°C). Place the cauliflower florets in a single layer in the air fryer basket. Air fry for 10-12 minutes, shaking the basket halfway through, until the cauliflower is tender and slightly browned.

2. **Cook the Beef:** Heat 1 tablespoon of oil in a large skillet over medium heat. Add the ground beef and cook until browned, breaking it up with a spoon. Drain any excess grease.

3. **Sauté Onions and Garlic:** Add the chopped onion and minced garlic to the skillet. Sauté for 2-3 minutes, until softened.

4. **Combine Ingredients:** Stir in the cream of mushroom soup, heavy cream, sour cream, Dijon mustard, thyme salt, and pepper. Bring the mixture to a simmer, stirring constantly.

5. **Assemble and Cook:** Add the cooked ground beef mixture and cauliflower rice to the air fryer basket. Toss gently to combine. Air fry for 5-7 minutes, shaking the basket once or twice during cooking, until the stroganoff is heated through.

6. **Serve:** Garnish with chopped fresh parsley, if desired. Serve hot and enjoy!

Nutritional Information (per serving): Calories: 520, Protein: 35g, Carbohydrates: 9g, Fat: 34g, Fiber: 4g, Cholesterol: 100mg, Sodium: 600mg, Potassium: 500mg

10.6 Air Fryer Keto Steak Fajitas
Yield: 2 servings **Prep Time:** 10 minutes **Cook Time:** 10-12 minutes

Ingredients:

- 1 (8-ounce) sirloin steak, cut into thin strips
- 1 tablespoon olive oil
- 1/2 teaspoon fajita seasoning

- 1 red bell pepper, sliced
- 1 green bell pepper, sliced
- 1/2 onion, sliced
- 1/4 cup chopped cilantro

Optional Ingredients:

- 1/4 cup diced avocado
- 1/4 cup salsa

- 1/4 cup sour cream
- 1 tablespoon lime juice

Instructions:

1. **Prepare the steak:** Preheat your air fryer to 400°F (200°C). In a bowl, combine the steak strips, olive oil, and fajita seasoning. Toss to coat evenly.
2. **Air fry the steak:** Place the seasoned steak in the air fryer basket, ensuring they are not overcrowding. Air fry for 6-8 minutes, shaking the basket halfway through cooking, until the steak is cooked to your desired doneness.
3. **Air fry the vegetables:** While the steak is cooking, toss the bell peppers and onion with a drizzle of olive oil in a separate bowl. Place the vegetables in the air fryer basket and air fry for 4-6 minutes, shaking the basket halfway through cooking, until the vegetables are tender-crisp.
4. **Serve the fajitas:** Remove the steak and vegetables from the air fryer. Arrange the steak and vegetables on a platter and top with cilantro. Serve immediately with your favorite keto-friendly toppings, such as avocado, salsa, sour cream, and lime juice.

Nutritional Information (per serving): Calories: 400, Protein: 35g, Carbohydrates: 10g, Fats: 20g, Fiber: 5g, Cholesterol: 100mg, Sodium: 300mg, Potassium: 500mg

7. Fish Recipes

1.7 Crispy Keto Air Fryer Fish & Chips
Yield: 2 servings **Prep Time:** 15 minutes **Cook Time:** 15-20 minutes

Ingredients:

For the Fish:

- 2 (4-ounce) cod fillets or other white fish
- 1 tablespoon olive oil
- 1/2 teaspoon salt
- 1/4 teaspoon black pepper
- 1/4 teaspoon paprika (optional)
- 1 tablespoon lemon juice (optional)

For the Cauliflower "Chips":

- 1 head cauliflower, cut into 1/2-inch thick slices
- 1/4 cup grated Parmesan cheese
- 1/4 cup almond flour
- 1/4 cup melted butter
- 1 teaspoon garlic powder
- 1/2 teaspoon salt
- 1/4 teaspoon black pepper
- 1/4 teaspoon paprika (optional)

Instructions:

1. **Prepare the fish:** Preheat your air fryer to 400°F (200°C). Season the fish fillets with salt, pepper, paprika (optional), and lemon juice (optional).
2. **Prepare the cauliflower "chips":** In a bowl, combine the cauliflower slices, Parmesan cheese, almond flour, melted butter, garlic powder, salt, pepper, and paprika (optional). Toss to coat evenly.
3. **Air fry the cauliflower "chips":** Place the coated cauliflower slices in the air fryer basket, ensuring they are not overcrowding. Air fry for 10-12 minutes, shaking the basket halfway through cooking, until the cauliflower is golden brown and crispy.
4. **Air fry the fish:** While the cauliflower is cooking, place the fish fillets in the air fryer basket. Air fry for 6-minutes, flipping halfway through cooking, until the fish is cooked through and flaky.
5. **Serve:** Remove the fish and cauliflower from the air fryer. Arrange the fish and cauliflower on a platter and serve immediately.

Nutritional Information (per serving): Calories: 400, Protein: 30g, Carbohydrates: 10g, Fats: 25g, Fiber: 5g, Cholesterol: 100mg, Sodium: 300mg, Potassium: 400mg

2.7 Easy Keto Fish Tacos with Avocado Crema
Yield: 2 servings **Prep Time:** 10 minutes **Cook Time:** 10-12 minutes

Ingredients:

For the Fish:

- 2 (4-ounce) cod fillets or other white fish
- 1 tablespoon olive oil
- 1/2 teaspoon taco seasoning
- 1/4 teaspoon salt
- 1/4 teaspoon black pepper
- 1/4 cup chopped cilantro (optional)

For the Avocado Crema:

- 1 ripe avocado, mashed
- 1 tablespoon sour cream
- 1 tablespoon lime juice
- 1/4 teaspoon salt
- 1/4 teaspoon black pepper

For Serving:

- 4 lettuce leaves (or your preferred keto-friendly tortilla alternative)
- 1/4 cup diced red onion
- 1/4 cup diced tomato
- 1/4 cup shredded cheese (cheddar, Monterey Jack, or your preference)
- 1 tablespoon chopped cilantro (optional)
- Hot sauce (optional)

Instructions:

1. **Prepare the fish:** Preheat your air fryer to 400°F (200°C). Combine the olive oil, taco seasoning, salt, and pepper in a bowl. Toss the fish fillets in the mixture to coat evenly.
2. **Air fry the fish:** Place the seasoned fish fillets in the air fryer basket, ensuring they are not overcrowding. Air fry for 6-8 minutes, flipping halfway through cooking, until the fish is cooked through and flaky.
3. **Make the avocado crema:** While the fish is cooking, combine the mashed avocado, sour cream, lime juice, salt, and pepper in a bowl. Stir until well combined.
4. **Assemble the tacos:** Remove the fish from the air fryer. Gently flake the fish with a fork. Place lettuce leaves (or your preferred tortilla alternative) on a plate and top with the flaked fish, avocado crema, diced red onion, diced tomato, shredded cheese, and chopped cilantro (optional). Add hot sauce to taste, if desired.

Nutritional Information (per serving): Calories: 450, Protein: 30g, Carbohydrates: 10g, Fats: 25g, Fiber: 5g, Cholesterol: 100mg, Sodium: 250mg, Potassium: 400mg

3.7 Air Fryer Keto Fish Sticks
Yield: 4 servings **Prep Time:** 10 minutes **Cook Time:** 8-10 minutes

Ingredients:

- 1 pound cod fillets, cut into 1-inch wide strips
- 1/4 cup almond flour
- 2 tablespoons grated Parmesan cheese
- 1/4 cup melted butter
- 1 teaspoon garlic powder
- 1/2 teaspoon salt
- 1/4 teaspoon black pepper
- 1/4 teaspoon paprika (optional)
- 1 tablespoon chopped fresh parsley (optional)

Instructions:

1. **Prepare the fish sticks:** Preheat your air fryer to 400°F (200°C). Combine the almond flour, Parmesan cheese, melted butter, garlic powder, salt, pepper, and paprika (optional) in a shallow dish. Dip each fish strip into the mixture, ensuring it is coated evenly.
2. **Air fry the fish sticks:** Place the coated fish sticks in the air fryer basket, ensuring they are not overcrowding. Air fry for 6-8 minutes, shaking the basket halfway through cooking, until the fish sticks are golden brown and cooked through.
3. **Serve:** Remove the fish sticks from the air fryer and serve immediately. Garnish with chopped parsley, if desired.

Nutritional Information (per serving): Calories: 200, Protein: 20g, Carbohydrates: 5g, Fats: 10g, Fiber: 2g, Cholesterol: 50mg, Sodium: 200mg, Potassium: 300mg

4.7 Spicy Keto Tuna Cakes
Yields: 4 servings **Prep time:** 10 minutes **Cook time:** 8-10 minutes

Ingredients:

- 1 (5-ounce) can tuna, drained and flaked
- 1/4 cup mayonnaise
- 1/4 cup chopped onion
- 1 tablespoon chopped celery
- 1 tablespoon chopped fresh parsley
- 1/4 teaspoon garlic powder
- 1/4 teaspoon onion powder

- 1/4 teaspoon smoked paprika
- 1/8 teaspoon cayenne pepper (optional, for extra spice)
- 1/4 teaspoon salt
- 1/8 teaspoon black pepper
- 1/4 cup grated Parmesan cheese
- 1 tablespoon olive oil (for brushing)

Instructions:

1. **Prepare the tuna mixture:** In a medium bowl, combine the flaked tuna, mayonnaise, onion, celery, parsley, garlic powder, onion powder, smoked paprika, cayenne pepper (optional), salt, and pepper. Mix well until all ingredients are evenly combined.
2. **Shape the tuna cakes:** Form the tuna mixture into four equal-sized patties, about 1-inch thick.
3. **Air fry the tuna cakes:** Preheat your air fryer to 400°F (200°C). Brush the tuna cakes lightly with olive oil and place them in the air fryer basket in a single layer, ensuring they're not overcrowded. Air fry for 8-10 minutes, flipping the tuna cakes halfway through cooking, until they are golden brown and cooked through.
4. **Serve:** Remove the tuna cakes from the air fryer and serve immediately. Top with grated Parmesan cheese (optional) and your favorite keto-friendly sides.

Nutritional Information per serving: Calories: 250, Protein: 25g, Carbohydrates: 3g, Fats: 15g, Fiber: 2g, Cholesterol: 80mg, Sodium: 300mg, Potassium: 400mg

5.7 Keto Fish & Veggie Skewers
Yield: 4 servings **Prep Time:** 15 minutes **Cook Time:** 10-12 minutes

Ingredients:

- 1 pound firm white fish (cod, tilapia, halibut), cut into 1-inch pieces
- 1 cup broccoli florets
- 1 cup cherry tomatoes
- 1/2 cup sliced bell peppers (any color)
- 1/4 cup chopped red onion
- 2 tablespoons olive oil

- 1 tablespoon lemon juice
- 1/2 teaspoon salt
- 1/4 teaspoon black pepper
- 1/4 teaspoon garlic powder
- 1/4 teaspoon dried oregano
- 8-10 wooden skewers, soaked in water for 30 minutes

Instructions:

1. **Prepare the skewers:** Thread the fish, broccoli, tomatoes, bell peppers, and red onion onto the skewers.
2. **Marinate the skewers:** In a medium bowl, combine the olive oil, lemon juice, salt, pepper, garlic powder, and oregano. Pour the marinade over the skewers, ensuring they are well coated. Marinate for at least 30 minutes, or up to 2 hours, in the refrigerator.

3. **Air fry:** Preheat your air fryer to 400°F (200°C). Place the marinated skewers in the air fryer basket, ensuring they are not overlapping. Cook for 10-12 minutes, flipping halfway through, until the fish is cooked through and the vegetables are tender. You can use a meat thermometer to check the internal temperature of the fish, which should reach 145°F (63°C).
4. **Serve:** Serve the skewers immediately with a side of keto-friendly sauce, such as lemon aioli, pesto, or chimichurri.

Nutritional Information (Per Serving): Calories: 350, Protein: 30g, Carbohydrates: 5g, Fats: 15g, Fiber: 5g, Cholesterol: 80mg, Sodium: 200mg, Potassium: 400mg

6.7 Keto Fish Curry with Coconut Milk
Yields: 2 servings **Prep time:** 10 minutes **Cook time:** 15-20 minutes

Ingredients:

- 2 cod fillets (about 6 ounces each)
- 1 tablespoon olive oil
- 1/2 onion, chopped
- 1 clove garlic, minced
- 1/2 teaspoon ground ginger
- 1/4 teaspoon ground turmeric
- 1/4 teaspoon cayenne pepper (optional, adjust to your spice preference)

- 1/2 cup full-fat coconut milk
- 1/4 cup chicken broth
- 1 tablespoon lemon juice
- 1/4 teaspoon salt
- 1/8 teaspoon black pepper
- 1/4 cup chopped cilantro (for garnish)

Instructions:

1. **Prepare the fish:** Pat the cod fillets dry with paper towels.
2. **Marinate the fish:** Combine 1 tablespoon olive oil, 1/4 teaspoon salt, and 1/8 teaspoon black pepper in a small bowl. Marinate the cod fillets in this mixture for 10 minutes.
3. **Prepare the curry sauce:** In a small bowl, combine the chopped onion, minced garlic, ground ginger, turmeric, and cayenne pepper (if using).
4. **Air fry the fish:** Preheat your air fryer to 400°F (200°C). Place the marinated cod fillets in the air fryer basket, ensuring they don't overlap. Air fry for 8-10 minutes, flipping halfway through cooking to ensure even browning.
5. **Cook the curry sauce:** While the fish is air frying, heat the remaining 1 tablespoon olive oil in a small saucepan over medium heat. Add the onion mixture and cook for about 5 minutes, or until softened. Pour in the coconut milk, chicken broth, lemon juice, salt, and pepper. Bring to a simmer and cook for 5 minutes, stirring occasionally.
6. **Assemble the curry:** Once the fish is cooked through, remove it from the air fryer. Pour the curry sauce over the fish in the air fryer basket. Air fry for an additional 2-3 minutes to allow the sauce to thicken slightly.
7. **Serve:** Garnish with chopped cilantro and serve immediately.

Nutritional information per serving (estimated): Calories: 400, Protein: 30g, Carbohydrates: 10g, Fats: 20g, Fiber: Cholesterol: 100mg, Sodium: 500mg, Potassium: 450mg

7.7 Air Fryer Keto Fish Burgers
Yields: 4 servings **Prep time:** 10 minutes **Cook time:** 8-10 minutes

Ingredients:

- 1 pound ground white fish (cod, tilapia, or haddock work well)
- 1/4 cup finely chopped onion
- 1/4 cup finely chopped celery
- 1 tablespoon chopped fresh parsley
- 1 tablespoon mayonnaise
- 1 egg
- 1/4 teaspoon garlic powder
- 1/4 teaspoon salt
- 1/8 teaspoon black pepper
- 1/4 cup shredded cheddar cheese (optional)
- 4 slices of avocado (optional)

Instructions:

1. **Combine ingredients:** In a large bowl, combine the ground fish, chopped onion, celery, parsley, mayonnai egg, garlic powder, salt, and pepper. Mix thoroughly with your hands, ensuring the ingredients are well combined.
2. **Form patties:** Divide the fish mixture into 4 equal portions and shape them into patties about 1/2 inch thick
3. **Add cheese (optional):** If desired, place a small amount of shredded cheddar cheese in the center of each patty.
4. **Air fry:** Preheat your air fryer to 400°F (200°C). Place the fish patties in the air fryer basket, ensuring they don't overlap. Air fry for 8-10 minutes, flipping halfway through cooking to ensure even browning and cooking.
5. **Serve:** Remove the fish patties from the air fryer and serve on lettuce wraps, avocado slices, or keto-friendl buns (if desired). Top with your favorite keto-friendly burger toppings, such as sliced tomato, pickles, or keto-friendly mustard.

Nutritional information per serving (estimated): Calories: 300, Protein: 30g, Carbohydrates: 5g, Fats: 15g, Fiber: 2g, Cholesterol: 100mg, Sodium: 400mg, Potassium: 400mg

8.7 Spicy Keto Fish Tacos with Mango Salsa
Yields: 2 servings **Prep time:** 10 minutes **Cook time:** 10-12 minutes

Ingredients:

- 2 cod fillets (about 6 ounces each)
- 1 tablespoon olive oil
- 1 teaspoon taco seasoning
- 1/4 teaspoon cayenne pepper (optional, adjust to your spice preference)
- 1/2 ripe mango, diced
- 1/4 red onion, diced
- 1/4 cup chopped cilantro
- 1 tablespoon lime juice
- 1/4 teaspoon salt
- 1/8 teaspoon black pepper
- 4 lettuce leaves (or keto-friendly tortillas, if desired)

Instructions:

1. **Prepare the fish:** Pat the cod fillets dry with paper towels.
2. **Marinate the fish:** Combine 1 tablespoon olive oil, taco seasoning, and cayenne pepper (if using) in a sm: bowl. Marinate the cod fillets in this mixture for 10 minutes.

3. **Make the mango salsa:** In a small bowl, combine the diced mango, red onion, cilantro, lime juice, salt, and pepper. Mix well and set aside.
4. **Air fry the fish:** Preheat your air fryer to 400°F (200°C). Place the marinated cod fillets in the air fryer basket, ensuring they don't overlap. Air fry for 10-12 minutes, flipping halfway through cooking to ensure even browning and cooking.
5. **Assemble the tacos:** Once the fish is cooked through, flake it with a fork. Divide the fish between the lettuce leaves (or keto-friendly tortillas) and top with the mango salsa.

utritional information per serving (estimated): Calories: 350, Protein: 30g, Carbohydrates: 10g, Fats: 15g, Fiber: , Cholesterol: 100mg, Sodium: 400mg, Potassium: 450mg

9.7 Keto Fish & Chips with Cauliflower Mash
Yields: 2 servings **Prep time:** 10 minutes **Cook time:** 15-20 minutes

Ingredients:

For the Halibut:

-   2 halibut fillets (about 6 ounces each)
-   1 tablespoon olive oil
-   1/4 teaspoon salt
-   1/8 teaspoon black pepper
-   1 tablespoon lemon juice (optional)
-   1 tablespoon chopped fresh dill (optional)

For the Cauliflower Mash:

-   1 head cauliflower, cut into florets
-   1/4 cup heavy cream
-   1 tablespoon butter
-   1/4 teaspoon salt
-   1/8 teaspoon black pepper
-   1/4 teaspoon garlic powder (optional)

Instructions:

1. **Prepare the halibut:** Pat the halibut fillets dry with paper towels. Drizzle 1/2 tablespoon olive oil over each fillet, and season with salt, pepper, lemon juice (optional), and chopped dill (optional).
2. **Prepare the cauliflower mash:** Steam or boil the cauliflower florets until tender, about 10-12 minutes. Drain well and transfer to a food processor. Add the heavy cream, butter, salt, pepper, and garlic powder (if using). Pulse until smooth.
3. **Air fry the halibut:** Preheat your air fryer to 400°F (200°C). Place the seasoned halibut fillets in the air fryer basket, ensuring they don't overlap. Air fry for 10-12 minutes, flipping halfway through cooking to ensure even browning and cooking.
4. **Serve:** Once the halibut is cooked through (it should flake easily with a fork), remove it from the air fryer. Serve the halibut with the cauliflower mash.

utritional information per serving (estimated): Calories: 400, Protein: 35g, Carbohydrates: 10g, Fats: 20g, Fiber: , Cholesterol: 100mg, Sodium: 350mg, Potassium: 450mg

10.7 Keto Salmon with Roasted Vegetables
Yields: 2 servings **Prep time:** 10 minutes **Cook time:** 15-20 minutes

Ingredients:

- 2 salmon fillets (about 6 ounces each)
- 1 tablespoon olive oil
- 1/2 teaspoon salt
- 1/4 teaspoon black pepper
- 1 cup broccoli florets
- 1 cup cauliflower florets
- 1/2 cup sliced zucchini
- 1/2 cup sliced bell pepper
- 1 tablespoon chopped fresh parsley (optional)

Instructions:

1. **Prepare the salmon:** Pat the salmon fillets dry with paper towels. Drizzle with olive oil and season with sa and pepper.
2. **Prepare the vegetables:** In a large bowl, toss the broccoli florets, cauliflower florets, sliced zucchini, and sliced bell pepper with 1 tablespoon olive oil, salt, and pepper.
3. **Air fry the salmon and vegetables:** Preheat your air fryer to 400°F (200°C). Place the seasoned salmon fillets in the air fryer basket and the vegetables in a separate basket or on a baking sheet that fits inside the a fryer. Air fry the salmon for 8-10 minutes, or until cooked through (it should flake easily with a fork). Air f the vegetables for 10-12 minutes, or until tender and slightly browned.
4. **Serve:** Transfer the cooked salmon and vegetables to plates and garnish with chopped fresh parsley (optional).

Nutritional information per serving (estimated): Calories: 450, Protein: 35g, Carbohydrates: 12g, Fats: 25g, Fib 4g, Cholesterol: 100mg, Sodium: 500mg, Potassium: 450m

11.7 Keto Steak Salad with Blue Cheese Dressing
Yield: 2 servings **Prep time:** 10 minutes **Cook time:** 10-12 minutes

Ingredients:

For the steak:

- 2 (4-ounce) sirloin steaks
- 1/2 teaspoon salt
- 1/4 teaspoon black pepper
- 1 tablespoon olive oil

For the blue cheese dressing:

- 1/4 cup crumbled blue cheese
- 1/4 cup mayonnaise
- 1 tablespoon sour cream
- 1 tablespoon lemon juice
- 1 clove garlic, minced
- 1/4 teaspoon Dijon mustard
- Salt and pepper to taste

For the salad:

- 1 cup mixed greens
- 1/4 cup chopped red onion
- 1/4 cup chopped walnuts (optional)
- 1/4 cup chopped fresh parsley

Instructions:

1. **Air fry the steak:** Preheat your air fryer to 400°F (200°C). Season the steaks with salt and pepper. Drizzle with olive oil and place in the air fryer basket. Cook for 10-12 minutes, flipping halfway through, until the steak reaches your desired level of doneness. Let the steak rest for a few minutes before slicing it.
2. **Make the blue cheese dressing:** In a small bowl, combine the blue cheese, mayonnaise, sour cream, lemon juice, minced garlic, Dijon mustard, salt, and pepper. Mix well until smooth.
3. **Assemble the salad:** Divide the mixed greens between two plates. Top each serving with sliced steak, chopped red onion, chopped walnuts (if using), and chopped parsley. Drizzle with blue cheese dressing.

Nutritional Information (per serving): Calories: 600, Protein: 40g, Carbohydrates: 5g, Fats: 40g, Fiber: 4g, Cholesterol: 150mg, Sodium: 500mg, Potassium: 500mg

12.7 Air Fryer Roasted Salmon Salad

Yield: 2 servings **Prep time:** 10 minutes **Cook time:** 8-10 minutes

Ingredients:

For the salmon:

- 2 (4-ounce) salmon fillets
- 1/2 teaspoon salt
- 1/4 teaspoon black pepper
- 1 tablespoon olive oil
- 1 tablespoon lemon juice

For the lemon dill dressing:

- 1/4 cup olive oil
- 2 tablespoons lemon juice
- 1 tablespoon chopped fresh dill
- 1/4 teaspoon Dijon mustard
- Salt and pepper to taste

For the salad:

- 1 cup mixed greens
- 1/4 cup chopped cucumber
- 1/4 cup cherry tomatoes, halved
- 1/4 cup sliced red onion
- 1/4 cup crumbled feta cheese

Instructions:

1. **Preheat the air fryer:** Set your air fryer to 400°F (200°C) and allow it to preheat for 3-5 minutes.
2. **Prepare the salmon:** Season the salmon fillets with salt, pepper, olive oil, and lemon juice. Place the salmon fillets in the air fryer basket, skin side down. Air fry for 8-10 minutes, or until the salmon is cooked through and flakes easily with a fork.
3. **Make the lemon dill dressing:** In a small bowl, whisk together the olive oil, lemon juice, chopped dill, Dijon mustard, salt, and pepper until well combined.
4. **Assemble the salad:** Divide the mixed greens between two plates. Top each serving with flaked salmon, chopped cucumber, cherry tomatoes, sliced red onion, crumbled feta cheese, and drizzle with lemon dill dressing.

Nutritional Information (per serving): Calories: 500, Protein: 35g, Carbohydrates: 5g, Fats: 30g, Fiber: 3g, Cholesterol: 120mg, Sodium: 300mg, Potassium: 500mg

13.7 Crispy Air Fryer Mackerel with Lemon and Dill
Yield: 2 servings **Prep Time:** 10 minutes **Cook Time:** 8-10 minutes

Ingredients:

- 2 mackerel fillets (about 6 oz each)
- 1 tablespoon olive oil
- 1 tablespoon lemon juice
- 1 tablespoon chopped fresh dill
- Salt and black pepper to taste
- Optional: 1/4 teaspoon garlic powder

Instructions:

1. **Prepare the mackerel:** Pat the mackerel fillets dry with paper towels.
2. **Season the fish:** In a small bowl, whisk together olive oil, lemon juice, dill, salt, pepper, and optional garlic powder.
3. **Marinate the mackerel:** Drizzle the marinade over the mackerel fillets, ensuring both sides are evenly coated.
4. **Air Fry:** Preheat your air fryer to 400°F (200°C). Place the mackerel fillets in the air fryer basket, ensuring they are not overcrowded.
5. **Cook:** Air fry for 8-10 minutes, or until the fish is cooked through and flaky. You may need to shake the basket halfway through cooking for even browning.
6. **Serve:** Remove the mackerel from the air fryer and serve immediately.

Nutritional Information per Serving: Calories: 250, Protein: 25g, Carbohydrates: 1g, Fat: 15g, Fiber: 0g, Cholesterol: 80mg, Sodium: 150mg, Potassium: 350mg

14.7 Sardines: Air Fryer Sardines with Garlic and Herbs
Yield: 2 servings **Preparation time:** 5 minutes **Cook time:** 8-10 minutes

Ingredients:

- 1 can (4 oz) sardines in olive oil, drained (about 6-8 sardines)
- 1 tablespoon olive oil
- 2 cloves garlic, minced
- 1/4 teaspoon dried oregano
- 1/4 teaspoon dried thyme
- Salt and freshly ground black pepper to taste
- 1 tablespoon fresh parsley, chopped (optional)
- 1/4 teaspoon red pepper flakes (optional)

Instructions:

1. **Preheat:** Preheat your air fryer to 400°F (200°C).
2. **Prepare Sardines:** Pat the sardines dry with paper towels.
3. **Marinade:** In a small bowl, combine the olive oil, minced garlic, oregano, thyme, salt, and pepper. Toss the sardines in the marinade, ensuring they are evenly coated.
4. **Air Fry:** Place the sardines in the air fryer basket in a single layer, leaving some space between each sardine. Air fry for 8-10 minutes, shaking the basket halfway through to ensure even cooking.
5. **Finish:** Remove the sardines from the air fryer and sprinkle with chopped parsley and red pepper flakes, if desired.

Nutritional Information Per Serving: Calories: 250, Protein: 15 grams, Carbohydrates: 1 gram, Fat: 18 grams, Fiber: 1 gram, Cholesterol: 80 milligrams, Sodium: 400 milligrams, Potassium: 200 milligrams

1.8 Crispy Keto Air Fryer Tofu Scramble
Yield: 2 servings Prep Time: 10 minutes Cook Time: 10-12 minutes

Ingredients:

- 1 block extra firm tofu, drained and crumbled
- 1 tablespoon olive oil
- 1/4 cup chopped onion
- 1/4 cup chopped bell pepper (red, green, or yellow)
- 1/4 cup chopped mushrooms

- 1/4 cup shredded cheddar cheese
- 1 teaspoon garlic powder
- 1/2 teaspoon salt
- 1/4 teaspoon black pepper
- 1/4 teaspoon paprika (optional)
- 1/4 cup chopped fresh cilantro (optional)

Instructions:

1. **Prepare the tofu:** Preheat your air fryer to 400°F (200°C). In a bowl, combine the crumbled tofu, olive oil, garlic powder, salt, pepper, and paprika (optional). Toss to coat evenly.
2. **Air fry the tofu:** Place the coated tofu in the air fryer basket, ensuring it is spread out in a single layer. Air fry for 5-7 minutes, stirring halfway through cooking, until the tofu is golden brown and crispy.
3. **Cook the vegetables:** While the tofu is cooking, heat a skillet over medium heat. Add the chopped onion, bell pepper, and mushrooms. Cook for 5-7 minutes, stirring occasionally, until the vegetables are tender-crisp.
4. **Assemble the scramble:** Remove the tofu from the air fryer and transfer it to a bowl. Add the cooked vegetables, shredded cheese, and chopped cilantro (optional). Toss to combine.
5. **Serve:** Serve the tofu scramble immediately.

Nutritional Information (per serving): Calories: 300, Protein: 20g, Carbohydrates: 5g, Fats: 15g, Fiber: 3g, Cholesterol: 20mg, Sodium: 300mg, Potassium: 400mg

2.8 Easy Keto Vegetable Curry
Yields: 4 servings Prep time: 15 minutes Cook time: 15-20 minutes

Ingredients:

- **For the Vegetables:**
  - 1 tablespoon olive oil
  - 1 cup broccoli florets
  - 1 cup cauliflower florets
  - 1 cup sliced carrots
  - 1 cup sliced zucchini
  - 1 cup sliced bell peppers (any color)
  - 1/2 cup sliced mushrooms
  - 1/2 teaspoon salt
  - 1/4 teaspoon black pepper
- **For the Curry Sauce:**
  - 1 tablespoon olive oil
  - 1 onion, finely chopped
  - 2 cloves garlic, minced
  - 1 (14-ounce) can full-fat coconut milk
  - 1 tablespoon curry powder
  - 1/2 teaspoon ground cumin
  - 1/4 teaspoon turmeric
  - 1/4 teaspoon salt
  - 1/8 teaspoon black pepper
  - Optional: 1/4 teaspoon red pepper flakes for a spicy kick
  - Optional: 1/4 cup chopped cilantro for garnish

Instructions:

1. **Prepare the vegetables:** In a large bowl, toss the broccoli, cauliflower, carrots, zucchini, bell peppers, and mushrooms with the olive oil, salt, and pepper.
2. **Air fry the vegetables:** Preheat your air fryer to 400°F (200°C). Divide the vegetables evenly between two batches and air fry for 8-10 minutes per batch, shaking the basket halfway through cooking, until the vegetables are tender-crisp and slightly browned.
3. **Make the curry sauce:** While the vegetables are air frying, heat the olive oil in a medium saucepan over medium heat. Add the chopped onion and cook until softened, about 5 minutes. Stir in the minced garlic and cook for another minute.
4. **Combine the ingredients:** Add the coconut milk, curry powder, cumin, turmeric, salt, and pepper to the saucepan. Bring to a simmer and cook for 10-15 minutes, or until the sauce has thickened slightly.
5. **Combine and serve:** Add the cooked vegetables to the sauce and stir to combine. Simmer for another 2-3 minutes to allow the flavors to blend. Serve immediately, garnished with chopped cilantro and red pepper flakes (optional).

Nutritional Information per serving: Calories: 350, Protein: 10g, Carbohydrates: 15g, Fats: 20g, Fiber: 8g, Cholesterol: 20mg, Sodium: 350mg, Potassium: 600mg

3.8 Air Fryer Keto Vegetable Fritters
Yield: 6 servings **Prep Time:** 15 minutes **Cook Time:** 15 minutes

Ingredients:

- 1 cup grated zucchini (about 1 medium zucchini)
- 1 cup grated yellow squash (about 1 medium squash)
- 1/2 cup finely chopped onion (about 1 small onion)
- 1/4 cup chopped fresh parsley
- 4 large eggs

- 1/4 cup shredded cheddar cheese
- 1/4 cup almond flour
- 1/4 teaspoon garlic powder
- 1/4 teaspoon salt
- 1/4 teaspoon black pepper
- 1 tablespoon olive oil (optional, for greasing the air fryer basket)

Optional Ingredients:

- 1/4 cup grated Parmesan cheese
- 1 tablespoon chopped fresh chives

- 1/2 teaspoon dried oregano

Instructions:

1. **Prepare the vegetables:** Grate the zucchini and yellow squash using a box grater or food processor. Chop onion and parsley finely.
2. **Combine ingredients:** In a large bowl, whisk together the eggs, almond flour, garlic powder, salt, and pepper. Add the grated zucchini, yellow squash, onion, parsley, and cheddar cheese. Stir well to combine.
3. **Optional additions:** If using, add the grated Parmesan cheese, chives, and oregano to the mixture.
4. **Preheat the air fryer:** Preheat your air fryer to 400°F (200°C) for 5 minutes.
5. **Grease the basket:** If desired, lightly grease the air fryer basket with olive oil.
6. **Form fritters:** Using a spoon, drop the fritter mixture into the preheated air fryer basket in even portions. Leave some space between each fritter to allow for air circulation.
7. **Air fry:** Air fry the fritters for 10-12 minutes, shaking the basket halfway through cooking to ensure even browning.

8. **Check for doneness:** The fritters are done when they are golden brown and cooked through.
9. **Serve:** Serve the Air Fryer Keto Vegetable Fritters immediately, or store in an airtight container in the refrigerator for up to 3 days.

Nutritional Information (per serving): Calories: 230, Protein: 14 grams, Carbohydrates: 5 grams, Fats: 16 grams, Fiber: 2 grams, Cholesterol: 90 mg, Sodium: 230 mg, Potassium: 280 mg

4.8 Keto Cauliflower Rice Pilaf
Yield: 4 servings **Prep Time:** 10 minutes **Cook Time:** 10-12 minutes

Ingredients:

- 1 large head of cauliflower, cut into small florets
- 1 tablespoon olive oil
- 1/4 cup chopped onion
- 1/4 cup chopped celery
- 1/4 teaspoon salt
- 1/8 teaspoon black pepper
- 1/4 teaspoon garlic powder
- 1/4 teaspoon onion powder
- Optional: 1 tablespoon chopped fresh parsley
- Optional: 1/4 teaspoon dried thyme
- Optional: 1/4 cup crumbled feta cheese

Instructions:

1. **Prepare the cauliflower:** Pulse the cauliflower florets in a food processor until they resemble rice grains.
2. **Air fry the cauliflower rice:** Preheat your air fryer to 400°F (200°C). Toss the cauliflower rice with olive oil, salt, pepper, garlic powder, and onion powder in a bowl. Spread the cauliflower rice in a single layer in the air fryer basket. Cook for 8-10 minutes, shaking the basket halfway through, until the cauliflower rice is lightly browned and tender.
3. **Sauté the vegetables:** While the cauliflower rice is cooking, heat a skillet over medium heat. Add the chopped onions and celery and sauté for 5-7 minutes, or until softened.
4. **Combine and serve:** Combine the cooked cauliflower rice with the sautéed onions and celery. Stir in the optional parsley, thyme, and feta cheese. Serve immediately.

Nutritional Information (Per Serving): Calories: 150, Protein: 5g, Carbohydrates: 5g, Fats: 8g, Fiber: 4g, Cholesterol: 10mg, Sodium: 100mg, Potassium: 200mg

5.8 Crispy Air Fryer Tofu Nuggets with Sweet Chili Sauce
Yield: 4 servings **Prep Time:** 15 minutes **Cook Time:** 15 minutes

Ingredients:

- 1 block (14 oz) extra-firm tofu, drained and pressed
- 1/4 cup almond flour
- 1/4 cup grated parmesan cheese
- 1 tablespoon avocado oil
- 1 teaspoon garlic powder
- 1/2 teaspoon onion powder
- 1/4 teaspoon salt
- 1/4 teaspoon black pepper
- 1/4 cup erythritol, for coating (optional)
- 1/4 cup keto-friendly sweet chili sauce (store-bought or homemade)

Instructions:

1. **Prepare the tofu:** Crumble the pressed tofu into a medium bowl.
2. **Create the breading:** In a separate bowl, combine almond flour, parmesan cheese, avocado oil, garlic powder, onion powder, salt, and pepper.
3. **Coat the tofu:** Add the crumbled tofu to the breading mixture and mix well until all pieces are evenly coate
4. **Optional: Sugar-free coating:** If using erythritol, sprinkle a thin layer over the coated tofu, ensuring all pieces are dusted.
5. **Air fry:** Preheat your air fryer to 400°F (200°C). Place the coated tofu nuggets in the air fryer basket, ensuring they are spread out in a single layer. Air fry for 10 minutes, shaking the basket halfway through to ensure even cooking.
6. **Crisp and finish:** Increase the temperature to 425°F (220°C) and air fry for another 5 minutes, or until the tofu nuggets are golden brown and crispy.
7. **Serve:** Serve hot with your favorite keto-friendly sweet chili sauce.

Nutritional Information (per serving): Calories: 240, Protein: 18g, Carbohydrates: 5g, Fat: 15g, Fiber: 2g, Cholesterol: 15mg, Sodium: 250mg, Potassium: 200mg

6.8 Creamy Keto Spinach & Artichoke Dip
Yields: 4 servings **Prep Time:** 10 minutes **Cook Time:** 10 minutes

Ingredients:

- 1 (14-ounce) can artichoke hearts, drained and chopped
- 1 (10-ounce) package frozen chopped spinach, thawed and squeezed dry
- 1/2 cup cream cheese, softened
- 1/4 cup grated Parmesan cheese
- 1/4 cup heavy cream
- 1/4 cup mayonnaise
- 2 cloves garlic, minced
- 1/4 teaspoon salt
- 1/4 teaspoon black pepper
- 1/4 cup shredded mozzarella cheese (optional, for topping)

Instructions:

1. **Combine ingredients:** In a medium bowl, combine the artichoke hearts, spinach, cream cheese, Parmesan cheese, heavy cream, mayonnaise, garlic, salt, and pepper. Mix thoroughly until well combined.
2. **Air fry:** Preheat your air fryer to 350°F (175°C). Transfer the spinach and artichoke mixture to an air fryer safe dish.
3. **Cook:** Air fry for 8-10 minutes, or until the dip is heated through and bubbly.
4. **Top and serve:** Sprinkle with shredded mozzarella cheese (optional) during the last 2 minutes of cooking added melty goodness. Serve immediately with keto-friendly dipping options like celery sticks, bell peppe slices, or keto bread.

Nutritional Information (per serving): Calories: 350, Protein: 15 grams, Carbohydrates: 5 grams, Fat: 28 grams Fiber: 2 grams, Cholesterol: 80 milligrams, Sodium: 400 milligrams, Potassium: 250 milligrams

7.8 Crispy Keto Zucchini Noodles with Pesto
Yield: 2 servings **Prep Time:** 10 minutes **Cook Time:** 10 minutes

Ingredients:

- 2 medium zucchini, spiralized into noodles
- 2 tablespoons olive oil
- 1/4 teaspoon salt
- 1/4 teaspoon black pepper
- 1/4 cup pesto (store-bought or homemade)
- 1/4 cup grated Parmesan cheese (optional)

Instructions:

1. **Prepare the zucchini:** Using a spiralizer, create long zucchini noodles.
2. **Toss with oil and seasonings:** Place the zucchini noodles in a large bowl. Add olive oil, salt, and pepper. Toss gently to coat evenly.
3. **Air fry:** Preheat your air fryer to 400°F (200°C). Place the zucchini noodles in the air fryer basket in a single layer.
4. **Cook and shake:** Air fry for 5-7 minutes, shaking the basket halfway through to ensure even cooking. The zucchini noodles should be slightly browned and crispy.
5. **Serve:** Remove from the air fryer and toss with pesto and Parmesan cheese (optional). Serve immediately.

Nutritional Information Per Serving: Calories: 320, Protein: 7 grams, Carbohydrates: 10 grams, Fat: 25 grams, Fiber: 3 grams, Cholesterol: 20 mg, Sodium: 200 mg, Potassium: 500 mg

8.8 Garlic Parmesan Keto Broccoli Bites
Yield: 4 servings **Prep Time:** 5 minutes **Cook Time:** 8-10 minutes

Ingredients:

- 1 head broccoli, cut into florets
- 2 tablespoons olive oil
- 2 tablespoons grated Parmesan cheese
- 1 teaspoon garlic powder
- 1/4 teaspoon salt
- 1/4 teaspoon black pepper

Instructions:

1. **Prepare the broccoli:** Preheat your air fryer to 400°F (200°C). In a large bowl, toss the broccoli florets with olive oil, Parmesan cheese, garlic powder, salt, and pepper. Make sure each floret is evenly coated.
2. **Air fry the broccoli bites:** Place the coated broccoli florets in the air fryer basket, ensuring they are not overcrowding. Air fry for 8-10 minutes, shaking the basket halfway through cooking, until the florets are tender and slightly crispy.
3. **Serve immediately:** Enjoy the warm, garlicky broccoli bites as a healthy snack, side dish, or topping for keto-friendly meals.

Nutritional Information (per serving): Calories: 150, Protein: 5g, Carbohydrates: 5g, Fats: 10g, Fiber: 3g, Cholesterol: 10mg, Sodium: 200mg, Potassium: 300mg

9.8 Spicy Air Fryer Tofu Scramble with Peppers and Onions
Yields: 2 servings **Prep Time:** 10 minutes **Cook Time:** 15 minutes

Ingredients:

- 14 oz extra-firm tofu, drained and pressed
- 1 tablespoon olive oil
- 1/2 teaspoon smoked paprika

- 1/2 red bell pepper, diced
- 1/2 green bell pepper, diced
- 1/2 medium onion, diced
- 1 teaspoon garlic powder

- 1/4 teaspoon cayenne pepper (optional, for extra spice)
- Salt and black pepper to taste
- 2 tablespoons chopped fresh cilantro (optional, for garnish)

Instructions:

1. **Prepare the tofu:** Crumble the pressed tofu into a large bowl using your hands or a fork.
2. **Combine ingredients:** Add olive oil, diced peppers, onion, garlic powder, smoked paprika, cayenne pepper (if using), salt, and pepper to the bowl with the tofu. Mix thoroughly to evenly coat all ingredients.
3. **Air fry:** Preheat your air fryer to 400°F (200°C). Place the tofu mixture in the air fryer basket, making sure it's in a single layer.
4. **Cook and shake:** Air fry for 10 minutes, shaking the basket halfway through to ensure even cooking.
5. **Check for doneness:** After 10 minutes, check the tofu for browning. If it's not yet cooked to your liking, continue air frying for another 2-3 minutes.
6. **Serve and garnish:** Remove the tofu scramble from the air fryer and serve immediately. Garnish with chopped cilantro for an extra burst of flavor.

Nutritional Information (per serving): Calories: 300, Protein: 25g, Carbohydrates: 6g, Fats: 15g, Fiber: 4g, Cholesterol: 0mg, Sodium: 250mg, Potassium: 500mg

10.8 Air Fryer Keto "Pasta" with Alfredo Sauce
Yield: 1 serving **Preparation Time:** 5 minutes **Cooking Time:** 5-7 minutes

Ingredients:

- 100g low-carb pasta alternative (such as shirataki noodles or zucchini noodles)
- 1/4 cup heavy cream

- 1/4 cup grated Parmesan cheese
- 1 tablespoon butter
- 1 clove garlic, minced (optional)
- Salt and black pepper to taste

Instructions:

1. Preheat your air fryer to 390°F (200°C).
2. Place the pasta alternative in the air fryer basket in a single layer. Cook for 3-5 minutes, shaking the basket halfway through, until slightly softened.
3. In a small bowl, whisk together the heavy cream, Parmesan cheese, butter, garlic (optional), salt, and black pepper.
4. Pour the sauce over the pasta alternative and mix well.
5. Continue air frying for an additional 2-4 minutes, until the sauce has thickened and the pasta is heated through.

Nutritional Information (per serving): Calories: 180, Protein: 10g, Carbohydrates: 10g (3g net carbs), Fats: 15g, Fiber: 2g, Cholesterol: 40mg, Sodium: 200mg, Potassium: 100mg

11.8 Keto Avocado Toast with Smoked Paprika
Yield: 1 serving **Prep time:** 5 minutes **Cook time:** 5-7 minutes

Ingredients:

- 1 slice (1/4 inch thick) keto bread (e.g., almond flour bread)
- 1/4 avocado, mashed
- 1/4 teaspoon smoked paprika
- Pinch of salt
- Pinch of black pepper
- Optional: 1/2 teaspoon chopped fresh chives or parsley
- Optional: 1 tablespoon crumbled feta cheese
- Optional: 1/4 teaspoon red pepper flakes

Instructions:

1. Preheat air fryer to 350°F (175°C).
2. Place the keto bread slice in the air fryer basket.
3. Air fry for 2-3 minutes, until lightly toasted.
4. Remove the bread from the air fryer and spread the mashed avocado evenly over the surface.
5. Sprinkle with smoked paprika, salt, and pepper.
6. Add optional toppings like chopped chives or parsley, crumbled feta cheese, and red pepper flakes.
7. Return the bread to the air fryer basket and cook for an additional 2-4 minutes, until the avocado is warmed through and the toppings are slightly melted (if using feta cheese).
8. Serve immediately.

Nutritional Information per Serving: Calories: 250-300 (depending on toppings), Protein: 10-15g, Carbohydrates: 5-15g (net carbs), Fat: 15-20g, Fiber: 3-5g, Cholesterol: 15-20mg, Sodium: 150-200mg, Potassium: 300-400mg

12.8 Air Fryer Keto Stuffed Bell Peppers
Yield: 2 servings **Prep time:** 15 minutes **Cook time:** 20-25 minutes

Ingredients:

- 2 medium bell peppers (any color)
- 1 tablespoon olive oil
- 1/2 cup diced onion
- 1/2 cup diced mushrooms
- 1/4 cup chopped fresh spinach
- 1/2 cup shredded cheddar cheese
- 1/4 cup cream cheese, softened
- 1/4 cup heavy cream
- 1 clove garlic, minced
- 1/4 teaspoon salt
- 1/4 teaspoon black pepper
- 1/4 teaspoon dried oregano (optional)
- 1/4 teaspoon red pepper flakes (optional, for a spicy kick)

Instructions:

1. **Prepare the bell peppers:** Cut the tops off the bell peppers and scoop out the seeds and membranes. Lightly drizzle the inside of the bell peppers with olive oil.
2. **Prepare the filling:** In a medium bowl, combine the diced onion, mushrooms, spinach, cheddar cheese, cream cheese, heavy cream, garlic, salt, pepper, oregano (if using), and red pepper flakes (if using). Mix well to combine.
3. **Stuff the peppers:** Divide the cheese mixture evenly between the two bell pepper halves. Place the stuffed bell peppers in the air fryer basket, standing upright if possible.
4. **Air fry:** Preheat the air fryer to 375°F (190°C). Air fry the stuffed peppers for 15-20 minutes, flipping them halfway through to ensure even cooking. The filling should be bubbly and the bell peppers should be tender. If necessary, continue cooking for an additional 5 minutes for extra browning.
5. **Serve:** Remove the stuffed bell peppers from the air fryer and let them cool slightly before serving.

Nutritional Information per Serving: Calories: 400-450, Protein: 20-25g, Carbohydrates: 10-15g (net carbs), Fat: 25-30g, Fiber: 5-7g, Cholesterol: 80-100mg, Sodium: 300-400mg, Potassium: 500-600mg

9. Soups

1.9 Keto Lentil Soup with Coconut Milk

Yield: 4 servings **Prep Time:** 15 minutes **Cook Time:** 30-35 minutes (for soup) + 3-5 minutes (for coconut flakes)

Ingredients:

For the Soup:

- 1 tablespoon olive oil
- 1/2 cup chopped onion
- 1/2 cup chopped celery
- 2 cloves garlic, minced
- 1/2 teaspoon salt
- 1/4 teaspoon black pepper
- 1/2 teaspoon cumin
- 1/4 teaspoon curry powder
- 1 cup red lentils, rinsed
- 4 cups beef broth
- 1 can (13.5 oz) full-fat coconut milk
- 1/4 cup chopped fresh cilantro (optional)
- 1/4 teaspoon red pepper flakes (optional, for spice)

For the Air-Fried Toasted Coconut Flakes:

- 1/2 cup unsweetened shredded coconut
- 1 tablespoon olive oil

Instructions:

1. **Prepare the soup:** Heat the olive oil in a large pot over medium heat. Sauté the onion and celery until softened, about 5 minutes. Add the garlic, salt, pepper, cumin, and curry powder. Cook for another minute, stirring constantly.
2. **Add lentils and broth:** Stir in the rinsed lentils and beef broth. Bring to a boil, then reduce heat to low, cover, and simmer for 25-30 minutes, or until the lentils are tender but still slightly firm.
3. **Finish the soup:** Stir in the coconut milk, cilantro (if using), and red pepper flakes (if using). Simmer for another 5 minutes, stirring occasionally, to allow flavors to meld.
4. **Prepare the toasted coconut flakes:** While the soup is simmering, preheat your air fryer to 350°F (175°C). Toss the shredded coconut with olive oil in a bowl.
5. **Air fry the coconut flakes:** Spread the coconut flakes in a single layer in the air fryer basket. Cook for 3-5 minutes, shaking the basket halfway through, until they are golden brown and toasted.
6. **Serve:** Ladle the soup into bowls and sprinkle with the toasted coconut flakes. Enjoy!

Nutritional Information (Per Serving): Calories: 350, Protein: 20g, Carbohydrates: 15g, Fats: 18g, Fiber: 10g, Cholesterol: 5mg, Sodium: 400mg, Potassium: 500mg

2.9 Creamy Keto Chicken and Broccoli Soup

Yield: 4 servings **Prep Time:** 15 minutes **Cook Time:** 25-30 minutes (for soup) + 5-7 minutes (for croutons)

Ingredients:

For the Soup:

- 1 tablespoon olive oil
- 1/2 cup chopped onion
- 1/2 cup chopped celery
- 1.5 cups chicken broth
- 1 cup heavy cream
- 1 cup shredded cheddar cheese

- 1/4 teaspoon salt
- 1/8 teaspoon black pepper
- 1/4 teaspoon garlic powder
- 1/4 teaspoon onion powder
- 2 cups chopped broccoli florets

- 1 cup cooked chicken, shredded
- 1/4 teaspoon dried thyme
- 1/4 teaspoon dried parsley
- Optional: 1-2 tablespoons sweetener (erythritol, stevia) to taste

or the Air-Fried Croutons:

- 4 slices keto-friendly bread (almond flour, coconut flour, or other low-carb bread)
- 1 tablespoon olive oil

- 1/4 teaspoon garlic powder
- 1/4 teaspoon Italian seasoning

Instructions:

1. **Prepare the soup:** In a large pot or Dutch oven, heat the olive oil over medium heat. Sauté the onion and celery until softened, about 5 minutes. Add the salt, pepper, garlic powder, and onion powder. Stir in the broccoli florets and cook for another 3-5 minutes.
2. **Simmer and blend:** Add the chicken broth, heavy cream, and cheddar cheese. Bring to a simmer and cook for 10 minutes, stirring occasionally, until the cheese is melted and the broccoli is tender. Remove from heat and use an immersion blender to blend the soup until smooth. You can also use a regular blender, but be careful with hot liquids.
3. **Add the chicken and seasonings:** Stir in the shredded chicken, thyme, and parsley. Taste and adjust seasonings, adding sweetener as desired.
4. **Prepare the croutons:** While the soup is simmering, preheat your air fryer to 375°F (190°C). Cut the keto-friendly bread into bite-sized cubes. Toss them in a bowl with olive oil, garlic powder, and Italian seasoning.
5. **Air fry the croutons:** Spread the crouton cubes in a single layer in the air fryer basket. Cook for 5-7 minutes, shaking the basket halfway through, until they are golden brown and crispy.
6. **Serve:** Ladle the soup into bowls and top with the air-fried croutons. Enjoy!

Nutritional Information (Per Serving): Calories: 400, Protein: 30g, Carbohydrates: 10g, Fats: 25g, Fiber: 5g, Cholesterol: 100mg, Sodium: 250mg, Potassium: 400mg

3.9 Spicy Keto Taco Soup

Yield: 4 servings **Prep Time:** 15 minutes **Cook Time:** 25-30 minutes (for soup) + 5-7 minutes (for tortilla strips)

Ingredients:

For the Soup:

- 1 tablespoon olive oil
- 1/2 cup chopped onion
- 1 (15-ounce) can black beans, rinsed and drained
- 1 (15-ounce) can diced tomatoes, undrained
- 1 (10-ounce) can diced green chilies, undrained
- 1 teaspoon chili powder
- 1/2 teaspoon cumin
- 1/4 teaspoon garlic powder
- 1/4 teaspoon onion powder

- 1/2 teaspoon smoked paprika
- 1/4 teaspoon cayenne pepper (adjust to taste)
- 1 (14.5-ounce) can diced tomatoes and green chilies, undrained
- 1.5 cups beef broth
- 1 cup heavy cream
- 1/2 cup shredded cheddar cheese
- 1/4 cup chopped cilantro (optional)
- 1/4 cup crumbled cotija cheese (optional, for topping)

For the Air-Fried Tortilla Strips:

- 4 small keto-friendly tortillas (almond flour, coconut flour, or other low-carb tortillas)
- 1 tablespoon olive oil
- 1/4 teaspoon chili powder
- 1/4 teaspoon cumin
- Pinch of salt

Instructions:

1. **Prepare the soup:** Heat the olive oil in a large pot over medium heat. Sauté the onion until softened, about minutes. Add the black beans, diced tomatoes, green chilies, chili powder, cumin, garlic powder, onion powder, smoked paprika, and cayenne pepper. Cook for 5 minutes, stirring occasionally.
2. **Simmer and blend:** Add the diced tomatoes and green chilies, beef broth, and heavy cream. Bring to a simmer and cook for 15 minutes, stirring occasionally. Use an immersion blender to blend the soup until slightly chunky. You can also use a regular blender, but be careful with hot liquids.
3. **Add cheese and seasonings:** Stir in the cheddar cheese, cilantro (if using), and additional seasonings as desired.
4. **Prepare the tortilla strips:** While the soup is simmering, preheat your air fryer to 400°F (200°C). Cut the tortillas into thin strips. Toss them in a bowl with olive oil, chili powder, cumin, and salt.
5. **Air fry the tortilla strips:** Spread the tortilla strips in a single layer in the air fryer basket. Cook for 5-7 minutes, shaking the basket halfway through, until they are golden brown and crispy.
6. **Serve:** Ladle the soup into bowls and top with the air-fried tortilla strips and crumbled cotija cheese (if using). Enjoy!

Nutritional Information (Per Serving): Calories: 450, Protein: 25g, Carbohydrates: 15g, Fats: 25g, Fiber: 10g, Cholesterol: 80mg, Sodium: 500mg, Potassium: 550mg

4.9 Keto Zuppa Toscana with Italian Sausage

Yield: 4 servings **Prep Time:** 15 minutes **Cook Time:** 25-30 minutes (for soup) + 5-7 minutes (for kale chips)

Ingredients:

For the Soup:

- 1 tablespoon olive oil
- 1 pound Italian sausage, casings removed
- 1/2 cup chopped onion
- 1/2 cup chopped celery
- 2 cloves garlic, minced
- 1/4 teaspoon salt
- 1/8 teaspoon black pepper
- 1/2 teaspoon dried oregano
- 1/4 teaspoon red pepper flakes (adjust to taste)
- 4 cups chicken broth
- 1 cup heavy cream
- 1 bunch kale, stems removed and leaves rough chopped
- 1/2 cup chopped escarole or spinach (optional)
- 1/4 cup grated Parmesan cheese
- Optional: 1-2 tablespoons sweetener (erythrito stevia) to taste

For the Air-Fried Kale Chips:

- 1 bunch kale, stems removed and leaves roughly chopped
- 1 tablespoon olive oil
- 1/4 teaspoon salt
- 1/4 teaspoon garlic powder
- 1/4 teaspoon red pepper flakes (optional)

Instructions:

1. **Prepare the soup:** Heat the olive oil in a large pot or Dutch oven over medium heat. Crumble the Italian sausage into the pot and cook until browned, about 5-7 minutes. Drain off any excess grease.
2. **Sauté vegetables:** Add the onion and celery to the pot and sauté until softened, about 5 minutes. Stir in the garlic, salt, pepper, oregano, and red pepper flakes. Cook for another minute, stirring constantly.
3. **Simmer and blend:** Add the chicken broth, heavy cream, and kale. Bring to a simmer and cook for 15 minutes, stirring occasionally, until the kale is wilted. Use an immersion blender to blend the soup until slightly chunky. You can also use a regular blender, but be careful with hot liquids.
4. **Add cheese and seasonings:** Stir in the Parmesan cheese and additional seasonings as desired.
5. **Prepare the kale chips:** While the soup is simmering, preheat your air fryer to 350°F (175°C). Toss the kale with the olive oil, salt, garlic powder, and red pepper flakes (optional) in a large bowl.
6. **Air fry the kale:** Spread the kale in a single layer in the air fryer basket, ensuring the leaves are not overlapping. Cook for 5-7 minutes, shaking the basket halfway through, until they are crispy and slightly browned.
7. **Serve:** Ladle the soup into bowls and top with the air-fried kale chips. Enjoy!

Nutritional Information (Per Serving): Calories: 500, Protein: 30g, Carbohydrates: 15g, Fats: 30g, Fiber: 8g, Cholesterol: 120mg, Sodium: 500mg, Potassium: 500mg

5.9 Keto French Onion Soup with Air Fryer Croutons

Yield: 4 servings **Prep Time:** 15 minutes **Cook Time:** 25-30 minutes (for soup) + 5-7 minutes (for croutons)

Ingredients:

For the Soup:

- 1 tablespoon olive oil
- 2 large onions, thinly sliced
- 1 tablespoon butter
- 1/4 teaspoon salt
- 1/8 teaspoon black pepper

- 1/2 teaspoon dried thyme
- 1/4 teaspoon dried rosemary
- 3 cups beef broth
- 1/2 cup grated Gruyère cheese
- 1/4 cup heavy cream

For the Air-Fried Croutons:

- 4 slices keto-friendly bread (almond flour, coconut flour, or other low-carb bread)

- 1 tablespoon olive oil
- 1/4 teaspoon garlic powder
- 1/4 teaspoon Italian seasoning

Instructions:

1. **Prepare the soup:** Heat the olive oil in a large pot or Dutch oven over medium heat. Add the sliced onions and cook, stirring occasionally, until they are softened and caramelized, about 20-25 minutes. The onions should be a deep golden brown color.
2. **Add seasonings and broth:** Stir in the butter, salt, pepper, thyme, and rosemary. Cook for another minute, stirring constantly. Add the beef broth. Bring the mixture to a simmer and cook for 15 minutes, allowing the flavors to meld.
3. **Blend and finish:** Use an immersion blender to partially blend the soup, leaving some texture. Stir in the Gruyère cheese and heavy cream. Simmer for 5 more minutes, or until the cheese is melted and the soup is smooth.

4. **Prepare the croutons:** While the soup is simmering, preheat your air fryer to 375°F (190°C). Cut the keto-friendly bread into bite-sized cubes. Toss them in a bowl with olive oil, garlic powder, and Italian seasoning

5. **Air fry the croutons:** Spread the crouton cubes in a single layer in the air fryer basket. Cook for 5-7 minute shaking the basket halfway through, until they are golden brown and crispy.

6. **Serve:** Ladle the soup into bowls and top with the air-fried croutons. Enjoy!

Nutritional Information (Per Serving): Calories: 450, Protein: 15g, Carbohydrates: 10g, Fats: 30g, Fiber: 3g, Cholesterol: 100mg, Sodium: 450mg, Potassium: 400mg

6.9 Keto Creamy Mushroom Soup

Yield: 4 servings **Prep Time:** 15 minutes **Cook Time:** 25-30 minutes (for soup) + 5-7 minutes (for croutons)

Ingredients:

For the Soup:

- 1 tablespoon olive oil
- 1 pound cremini mushrooms, sliced
- 1/2 cup chopped onion
- 2 cloves garlic, minced
- 1/4 teaspoon salt
- 1/8 teaspoon black pepper
- 1/2 teaspoon dried thyme
- 1/4 teaspoon dried rosemary

- 2 cups unsweetened almond milk (or other unsweetened plant-based milk)
- 1 cup heavy cream
- 1/2 cup grated Parmesan cheese
- 1 tablespoon chopped fresh parsley (optional)
- Optional: 1-2 tablespoons sweetener (erythritol stevia) to taste

For the Air-Fried Croutons:

- 4 slices keto-friendly bread (almond flour, coconut flour, or other low-carb bread)

- 1 tablespoon olive oil
- 1/4 teaspoon garlic powder
- 1/4 teaspoon Italian seasoning

Instructions:

1. **Prepare the soup:** Heat the olive oil in a large pot or Dutch oven over medium heat. Add the sliced mushrooms and cook, stirring occasionally, until they are softened and browned, about 10-15 minutes. The mushrooms should release their moisture and become slightly caramelized.

2. **Add seasonings and milk:** Stir in the onion and garlic. Cook for another minute, stirring constantly. Add salt, pepper, thyme, and rosemary. Cook for another minute, stirring constantly. Add the almond milk and bring the mixture to a simmer. Cook for 15 minutes, allowing the flavors to meld.

3. **Blend and finish:** Use an immersion blender to blend the soup until smooth. Stir in the heavy cream and Parmesan cheese. Simmer for 5 more minutes, or until the cheese is melted and the soup is creamy. Stir in parsley (if using).

4. **Prepare the croutons:** While the soup is simmering, preheat your air fryer to 375°F (190°C). Cut the keto friendly bread into bite-sized cubes. Toss them in a bowl with olive oil, garlic powder, and Italian seasonir

5. **Air fry the croutons:** Spread the crouton cubes in a single layer in the air fryer basket. Cook for 5-7 minu shaking the basket halfway through, until they are golden brown and crispy.

6. **Serve:** Ladle the soup into bowls and top with the air-fried croutons. Enjoy!

Nutritional Information (Per Serving): Calories: 350, Protein: 15g, Carbohydrates: 10g, Fats: 20g, Fiber: 3g, Cholesterol: 70mg, Sodium: 350mg, Potassium: 400mg

7.9 Air Fryer Keto Pumpkin Soup

Yield: 4 servings **Prep Time:** 15 minutes **Cook Time:** 25-30 minutes (for soup) + 5-7 minutes (for pumpkin seeds)

Ingredients:

For the Soup:

- 1 tablespoon olive oil
- 1 large onion, chopped
- 2 cloves garlic, minced
- 1/4 teaspoon salt
- 1/8 teaspoon black pepper
- 1/2 teaspoon ground ginger
- 1/4 teaspoon ground cinnamon
- 1/4 teaspoon ground nutmeg
- 1 (15-ounce) can pumpkin puree

- 2 cups unsweetened almond milk (or other unsweetened plant-based milk)
- 1 cup heavy cream
- 1/4 cup grated Parmesan cheese
- 1/4 cup chopped fresh sage (optional)
- Optional: 1-2 tablespoons sweetener (erythritol, stevia) to taste

For the Air-Fried Pumpkin Seeds:

- 1/2 cup pumpkin seeds
- 1 tablespoon olive oil
- 1/4 teaspoon salt

- 1/4 teaspoon garlic powder
- 1/4 teaspoon paprika (optional)

Instructions:

1. **Prepare the soup:** Heat the olive oil in a large pot or Dutch oven over medium heat. Add the onion and cook, stirring occasionally, until softened, about 5 minutes. Stir in the garlic, salt, pepper, ginger, cinnamon, and nutmeg. Cook for another minute, stirring constantly.
2. **Simmer and blend:** Add the pumpkin puree, almond milk, and heavy cream. Bring to a simmer and cook for 15 minutes, stirring occasionally, until the pumpkin puree is warmed through. Use an immersion blender to blend the soup until smooth. You can also use a regular blender, but be careful with hot liquids.
3. **Add cheese and seasonings:** Stir in the Parmesan cheese, sage (if using), and additional seasonings as desired.
4. **Prepare the pumpkin seeds:** While the soup is simmering, preheat your air fryer to 350°F (175°C). Rinse the pumpkin seeds and pat them dry. Toss them in a bowl with olive oil, salt, garlic powder, and paprika (optional).
5. **Air fry the pumpkin seeds:** Spread the pumpkin seeds in a single layer in the air fryer basket. Cook for 5-7 minutes, shaking the basket halfway through, until they are golden brown and crispy.
6. **Serve:** Ladle the soup into bowls and top with the air-fried pumpkin seeds. Enjoy!

Nutritional Information (Per Serving): Calories: 400, Protein: 15g, Carbohydrates: 15g, Fats: 25g, Fiber: 5g, Cholesterol: 80mg, Sodium: 400mg, Potassium: 450mg

8.9 Air Fryer Keto Chicken Noodle Soup

Yield: 4 servings **Prep Time:** 15 minutes **Cook Time:** 25-30 minutes (for soup) + 5-7 minutes (for noodles)

Ingredients:

For the Soup:

- 1 tablespoon olive oil
- 1 pound boneless, skinless chicken breasts, cut into bite-sized pieces
- 1 large onion, chopped
- 2 cloves garlic, minced
- 1/4 teaspoon salt
- 1/8 teaspoon black pepper

- 1/2 teaspoon dried thyme
- 1/4 teaspoon dried parsley
- 4 cups chicken broth
- 1 cup heavy cream
- 1/4 cup chopped fresh dill (optional)
- Optional: 1-2 tablespoons sweetener (erythritol, stevia) to taste

For the Air-Fried Shirataki Noodles:

- 1 (8-ounce) package shirataki noodles, drained and rinsed
- 1 tablespoon olive oil

- 1/4 teaspoon garlic powder
- 1/4 teaspoon Italian seasoning

Instructions:

1. **Prepare the soup:** Heat the olive oil in a large pot or Dutch oven over medium heat. Add the chicken and cook, stirring occasionally, until browned on all sides, about 5-7 minutes.
2. **Add vegetables and broth:** Stir in the onion and garlic. Cook for another minute, stirring constantly. Add salt, pepper, thyme, and parsley. Cook for another minute, stirring constantly. Add the chicken broth and bring the mixture to a simmer. Cook for 15 minutes, allowing the flavors to meld.
3. **Shred chicken and finish:** Remove the chicken from the pot and shred it with two forks. Return the shredded chicken to the pot. Stir in the heavy cream and dill (if using). Simmer for 5 more minutes, or until the soup heated through.
4. **Prepare the noodles:** While the soup is simmering, preheat your air fryer to 350°F (175°C). Toss the shirataki noodles with olive oil, garlic powder, and Italian seasoning in a bowl.
5. **Air fry the noodles:** Spread the shirataki noodles in a single layer in the air fryer basket. Cook for 5-7 minutes, shaking the basket halfway through, until they are slightly browned and crispy.
6. **Serve:** Ladle the soup into bowls and top with the air-fried shirataki noodles. Enjoy!

Nutritional Information (Per Serving): Calories: 450, Protein: 30g, Carbohydrates: 5g, Fats: 20g, Fiber: 3g, Cholesterol: 100mg, Sodium: 500mg, Potassium: 450mg

9.9 Keto Spinach and Artichoke Soup

Yield: 4 servings **Prep Time:** 15 minutes **Cook Time:** 25-30 minutes (for soup) + 5-7 minutes (for croutons)

Ingredients:

For the Soup:

- 1 tablespoon olive oil
- 1/2 cup chopped onion

- 1 (10-ounce) package frozen chopped spinach, thawed and squeezed dry

- 2 cloves garlic, minced
- 1/4 teaspoon salt
- 1/8 teaspoon black pepper
- 1/2 teaspoon dried oregano
- 1 (14-ounce) can artichoke hearts, drained and chopped

- 2 cups heavy cream
- 1/2 cup grated Parmesan cheese
- 1/4 cup chopped fresh basil (optional)
- Optional: 1-2 tablespoons sweetener (erythritol, stevia) to taste

or the Air-Fried Parmesan Croutons:

- 4 slices keto-friendly bread (almond flour, coconut flour, or other low-carb bread)
- 1 tablespoon olive oil

- 1/4 cup grated Parmesan cheese
- 1/4 teaspoon garlic powder
- 1/4 teaspoon Italian seasoning

structions:

1. **Prepare the soup:** Heat the olive oil in a large pot or Dutch oven over medium heat. Add the onion and cook, stirring occasionally, until softened, about 5 minutes. Stir in the garlic, salt, pepper, and oregano. Cook for another minute, stirring constantly.
2. **Simmer and blend:** Add the artichoke hearts and spinach. Cook for 5 minutes, stirring occasionally, until the spinach is heated through. Use an immersion blender to blend the soup until slightly chunky. You can also use a regular blender, but be careful with hot liquids.
3. **Add cream and cheese:** Stir in the heavy cream and Parmesan cheese. Bring to a simmer and cook for 10 minutes, stirring occasionally, until the cheese is melted and the soup is creamy.
4. **Add seasonings:** Stir in the basil (if using) and additional seasonings as desired.
5. **Prepare the croutons:** While the soup is simmering, preheat your air fryer to 375°F (190°C). Cut the keto-friendly bread into bite-sized cubes. Toss them in a bowl with olive oil, Parmesan cheese, garlic powder, and Italian seasoning.
6. **Air fry the croutons:** Spread the crouton cubes in a single layer in the air fryer basket. Cook for 5-7 minutes, shaking the basket halfway through, until they are golden brown and crispy.
7. **Serve:** Ladle the soup into bowls and top with the air-fried Parmesan croutons. Enjoy!

utritional Information (Per Serving): Calories: 450, Protein: 20g, Carbohydrates: 10g, Fats: 30g, Fiber: 4g, olesterol: 100mg, Sodium: 450mg, Potassium: 450mg

10.9 Spicy Keto Chili with Ground Beef
Yield: 4 servings **Prep Time:** 15 minutes **Cook Time:** 30-35 minutes (for chili) + 5-7 minutes (for jalapeños)

gredients:

r the Chili:

- 1 tablespoon olive oil
- 1 pound ground beef
- 1 large onion, chopped
- 2 cloves garlic, minced
- 1 (15-ounce) can black beans, rinsed and drained
- 1 (15-ounce) can kidney beans, rinsed and drained
- 1 (28-ounce) can crushed tomatoes, undrained

- 1 tablespoon chili powder
- 1 teaspoon cumin
- 1 teaspoon smoked paprika
- 1/2 teaspoon cayenne pepper (or to taste)
- 1/4 teaspoon salt
- 1/8 teaspoon black pepper
- 1 cup beef broth (optional)
- 1/4 cup chopped fresh cilantro (optional)

- 1 (14.5-ounce) can diced tomatoes and green chilies, undrained

For the Air-Fried Jalapeño Slices:

- 2 jalapeños, thinly sliced
- 1 tablespoon olive oil
- 1/4 teaspoon salt
- 1/4 teaspoon garlic powder
- 1/4 teaspoon smoked paprika (optional)

Instructions:

1. **Prepare the chili:** Heat the olive oil in a large pot or Dutch oven over medium heat. Add the ground beef a cook, breaking it up with a spoon, until browned, about 5-7 minutes. Drain off any excess grease.
2. **Sauté vegetables:** Add the onion and garlic to the pot and sauté until softened, about 5 minutes. Stir in the chili powder, cumin, paprika, cayenne pepper, salt, and black pepper. Cook for another minute, stirring constantly.
3. **Simmer and blend:** Add the black beans, kidney beans (optional), crushed tomatoes, diced tomatoes and green chilies, and beef broth (if using). Bring to a simmer and cook for 20 minutes, stirring occasionally. U an immersion blender to blend the chili until slightly chunky. You can also use a regular blender, but be careful with hot liquids.
4. **Add seasonings:** Stir in the cilantro (if using) and additional seasonings as desired.
5. **Prepare the jalapeño slices:** While the chili is simmering, preheat your air fryer to 400°F (200°C). Toss th jalapeño slices with the olive oil, salt, garlic powder, and smoked paprika (optional) in a bowl.
6. **Air fry the jalapeños:** Spread the jalapeño slices in a single layer in the air fryer basket. Cook for 5-7 minutes, shaking the basket halfway through, until they are crispy and slightly browned.
7. **Serve:** Ladle the chili into bowls and top with the air-fried jalapeño slices. Enjoy!

Nutritional Information (Per Serving): Calories: 550, Protein: 35g, Carbohydrates: 20g, Fats: 25g, Fiber: 10g, Cholesterol: 100mg, Sodium: 600mg, Potassium: 500mg

0. Desserts:

1.10 Keto Air Fryer Chocolate Chip Cookies
Yield: 12 cookies Prep Time: 10 minutes Cook Time: 6-8 minutes

Ingredients:

- 1/2 cup (1 stick) unsalted butter, softened
- 1/4 cup erythritol (or your preferred sugar substitute)
- 1/4 cup almond flour
- 1/4 cup coconut flour
- 1/4 teaspoon baking soda
- 1/4 teaspoon salt
- 1 teaspoon vanilla extract
- 1/4 cup sugar-free chocolate chips

Instructions:

1. **Preheat air fryer:** Preheat your air fryer to 350°F (175°C).
2. **Combine dry ingredients:** In a medium bowl, whisk together the almond flour, coconut flour, baking soda, and salt.
3. **Cream butter and sweetener:** In a separate bowl, cream together the softened butter and erythritol until light and fluffy. Beat in the vanilla extract.
4. **Mix wet and dry ingredients:** Gradually add the dry ingredients to the wet ingredients, mixing until just combined. Don't overmix.
5. **Fold in chocolate chips:** Gently fold in the sugar-free chocolate chips.
6. **Form cookies:** Drop rounded tablespoons of dough onto a parchment-lined air fryer basket.
7. **Air fry cookies:** Cook for 6-8 minutes, flipping the cookies halfway through, until golden brown and set.
8. **Cool cookies:** Let the cookies cool slightly in the air fryer basket before transferring them to a wire rack to cool completely.

Nutritional Information (Per Cookie): Calories: 150, Protein: 2g, Carbohydrates: 5g, Fats: 10g, Fiber: 2g, Cholesterol: 20mg, Sodium: 50mg, Potassium: 50mg

2.10 Keto Raspberry Cheesecake Bites
Yield: 12 servings Prep Time: 15 minutes Cook Time: 10-12 minutes

Ingredients:

- 1 (8 ounce) package cream cheese, softened
- 1/4 cup erythritol or keto-friendly sweetener
- 1 teaspoon vanilla extract
- 1/4 cup heavy cream
- 1/2 cup raspberries, fresh or frozen
- 1 tablespoon almond flour
- 1/4 teaspoon almond extract (optional)
- Pinch of salt

Equipment:

- Air fryer
- Medium bowl
- Small bowl
- Fork
- Measuring spoons and cups
- 12-cup muffin tin
- Parchment paper

Instructions:

1. **Prepare the base:** Preheat your air fryer to 350°F (175°C). Line a 12-cup muffin tin with parchment paper liners. In a medium bowl, combine the cream cheese, sweetener, vanilla extract, and heavy cream. Beat with fork until smooth and creamy.
2. **Assemble the bites:** Divide the cream cheese mixture evenly among the muffin cups. Top each with 4-5 raspberries. In a small bowl, mix the almond flour, almond extract (if using), and salt. Sprinkle a small amount of the mixture over the raspberries in each cup.
3. **Air fry:** Bake the cheesecake bites in the preheated air fryer for 10-12 minutes, or until the edges are golden brown and the center is set.
4. **Cool and serve:** Remove the bites from the air fryer and let them cool slightly before serving. Enjoy warm chilled.

Nutritional Information (per serving): Calories: 150, Protein: 3g, Carbohydrates: 3g, Fat: 12g, Fiber: 1g, Cholesterol: 30mg, Sodium: 50mg, Potassium: 100mg

3.10 Air Fryer Keto Brownies

Yield: 6 servings **Prep Time:** 5 minutes **Cook Time:** 10-12 minutes

Ingredients:

- 1/2 cup (1 stick) unsalted butter, melted
- 1/4 cup unsweetened cocoa powder
- 1/4 cup almond flour
- 1/4 cup erythritol or other keto-friendly sweetener
- 2 large eggs
- 1 teaspoon vanilla extract
- 1/4 teaspoon baking powder
- Pinch of salt
- **Optional:** 1/4 cup chopped nuts (walnuts, pecans, etc.)

Instructions:

1. **Preheat:** Preheat your air fryer to 350°F (175°C).
2. **Combine Ingredients:** In a medium bowl, whisk together the melted butter, cocoa powder, almond flour, erythritol, eggs, vanilla extract, baking powder, and salt.
3. **Stir in Nuts (optional):** If using, gently fold in the chopped nuts.
4. **Prepare Air Fryer:** Lightly spray your air fryer basket with non-stick cooking spray. Pour the brownie batter into the basket.
5. **Air Fry:** Cook for 10-12 minutes, or until a toothpick inserted into the center comes out with a few moist crumbs attached.
6. **Cool and Serve:** Let the brownies cool slightly in the air fryer before transferring to a wire rack to cool completely. Serve warm or at room temperature.

Nutritional Information (per serving): Calories: 250, Protein: 4 grams, Carbohydrates: 6 grams (2 grams net carbs), Fat: 20 grams, Fiber: 4 grams, Cholesterol: 50 mg, Sodium: 80 mg, Potassium: 100 mg

4.10 Creamy Keto Chocolate Mousse
Yields: 4 servings **Prep Time:** 10 minutes **Chill Time:** 2-3 hours

Ingredients:

- 1 cup heavy whipping cream
- 1/2 cup unsweetened cocoa powder
- 1/4 cup erythritol or other keto-friendly sweetener
- 1/4 cup unsweetened almond milk
- 1 teaspoon vanilla extract
- 1/4 teaspoon salt
- Optional: 1/4 cup chopped nuts for garnish
- Optional: 1 tablespoon unsweetened cocoa powder for dusting

Instructions:

1. **Chill the Cream:** Place the heavy whipping cream in a bowl and refrigerate for at least 30 minutes. This will help ensure the cream whips up nicely.
2. **Make the Chocolate Mixture:** In a separate bowl, whisk together the cocoa powder, erythritol, almond milk, vanilla extract, and salt until smooth.
3. **Whip the Cream:** Using an electric mixer, whip the chilled heavy whipping cream until stiff peaks form.
4. **Combine the Mixtures:** Gently fold the whipped cream into the chocolate mixture until just combined. Avoid overmixing, as this can deflate the mousse.
5. **Chill:** Transfer the mousse to individual serving dishes or ramekins. Cover and refrigerate for at least 2-3 hours, or until set.
6. **Serve:** Garnish with chopped nuts and dust with cocoa powder (optional) before serving.

Variations: For added richness and flavor, add a tablespoon of softened cream cheese or mascarpone cheese to the chocolate mixture.

Nutritional Information per Serving: Calories: 250, Protein: 3g, Carbohydrates: 8g, Fat: 20g, Fiber: 1g, Cholesterol: 40mg, Sodium: 80mg, Potassium: 150mg

5.10 Keto Lemon Bars with Almond Flour Crust
Yield: 8 servings **Prep Time:** 15 minutes **Cook Time:** 15 minutes

Ingredients:

Crust:
- 1 cup almond flour
- 1/4 cup melted coconut oil
- 1/4 cup erythritol
- 1/4 teaspoon salt
- 1/4 teaspoon vanilla extract

Filling:
- 1/2 cup unsalted butter, softened
- 1/2 cup erythritol
- 2 large eggs
- 1 tablespoon lemon zest
- 1/4 cup lemon juice
- 1/4 teaspoon salt

Optional Toppings:
- Fresh berries
- Whipped cream (keto-friendly)
- Lemon zest for garnish

Instructions:

1. **Prepare the Crust:** Preheat air fryer to 350°F (175°C). Combine almond flour, melted coconut oil, erythritol, salt, and vanilla extract in a medium bowl. Press the mixture evenly into the bottom of an 8-inch square baking pan lined with parchment paper.
2. **Bake the Crust:** Place the pan in the air fryer basket and cook for 5 minutes, or until the crust is lightly golden.
3. **Prepare the Filling:** While the crust bakes, combine softened butter, erythritol, eggs, lemon zest, lemon juice, and salt in a large bowl. Beat with an electric mixer until smooth and creamy.
4. **Assemble:** Pour the lemon filling over the baked crust.
5. **Air Fry:** Return the pan to the air fryer and cook for another 10 minutes, or until the filling is set.
6. **Cool & Slice:** Allow the lemon bars to cool completely in the air fryer basket. Once cooled, cut into 8 squares and serve.
7. **Add Toppings:** Top with your choice of fresh berries, whipped cream, and a sprinkle of lemon zest for a beautiful and flavorful presentation.

Nutritional Information (per serving): Calories: 270, Protein: 3g, Carbohydrates: 7g, Fat: 22g, Fiber: 2g, Cholesterol: 50mg, Sodium: 100mg, Potassium: 100mg

6.10 Air Fryer Keto Peanut Butter Cookies
Yield: 12 cookies **Prep Time:** 10 minutes **Cook Time:** 8-10 minutes

Ingredients:

- 1/2 cup almond flour
- 1/4 cup erythritol (or your preferred keto sweetener)
- 1/4 cup peanut butter (unsweetened, creamy)
- 1 large egg
- 1 teaspoon vanilla extract
- 1/4 teaspoon salt
- 1/4 cup chopped pecans or peanuts (optional)

Instructions:

1. Preheat your air fryer to 350°F (175°C).
2. In a medium bowl, combine the almond flour, erythritol, peanut butter, egg, vanilla extract, and salt. Mix until a dough forms.
3. If desired, stir in the chopped nuts.
4. Roll the dough into 12 equal-sized balls.
5. Place the cookie balls in the air fryer basket, leaving some space between each.
6. Air fry for 8-10 minutes, shaking the basket halfway through to ensure even cooking. The cookies should golden brown and set.
7. Let the cookies cool in the basket for a few minutes before transferring them to a wire rack to cool completely.

Nutritional Information per Cookie (Approximate): Calories: 165, Protein: 4g, Carbohydrates: 4g (1g net carb Fats: 15g, Fiber: 1g, Cholesterol: 20mg, Sodium: 80mg, Potassium: 100mg

7.10 Keto Pumpkin Spice Muffins

Yields: 6 servings **Prep Time:** 15 minutes **Cook Time:** 10-12 minutes

Ingredients:

- 1/2 cup almond flour
- 1/4 cup coconut flour
- 1/4 cup unsweetened shredded coconut
- 1/4 cup erythritol or other keto-friendly sweetener
- 1 teaspoon pumpkin pie spice
- 1/2 teaspoon baking soda

- 1/4 teaspoon salt
- 1/2 cup full-fat coconut milk
- 2 large eggs
- 1 tablespoon melted coconut oil
- 1/4 cup canned pumpkin puree
- 1/4 teaspoon vanilla extract
- **Optional:** 1/4 cup chopped pecans or walnuts for topping

Instructions:

1. **Preheat your air fryer to 350°F (175°C).**
2. **Combine dry ingredients:** In a large bowl, whisk together the almond flour, coconut flour, shredded coconut, erythritol, pumpkin pie spice, baking soda, and salt.
3. **Combine wet ingredients:** In a separate bowl, whisk together the coconut milk, eggs, melted coconut oil, pumpkin puree, and vanilla extract.
4. **Mix wet and dry ingredients:** Gradually add the wet ingredients to the dry ingredients, mixing until just combined. Do not overmix.
5. **Prepare muffins:** Line your air fryer basket with parchment paper or silicone liners. Divide the batter evenly among 6 muffin cups.
6. **Air fry:** Place the muffin cups in the preheated air fryer basket. Cook for 10-12 minutes, or until a toothpick inserted into the center comes out clean.
7. **Optional topping:** Sprinkle the muffin tops with chopped pecans or walnuts before cooking, if desired.
8. **Cool and serve:** Allow the muffins to cool slightly in the air fryer basket before transferring them to a wire rack to cool completely. Serve warm or at room temperature.

Nutritional Information: Calories: 250, Protein: 6g, Carbohydrates: 6g, Fats: 20g, Fiber: 4g, Cholesterol: 70mg, Sodium: 150mg, Potassium: 200mg

8.10 Keto Strawberry Shortcake with Coconut Cream

Yield: 4 servings **Prep time:** 10 minutes **Cook time:** 10-12 minutes

Ingredients:

- **Shortcake:**
    - 1 cup almond flour
    - 1/4 cup unsweetened shredded coconut
    - 1/4 cup erythritol or your preferred sweetener
    - 1/4 teaspoon baking powder
    - 1/4 teaspoon salt
    - 1/4 cup heavy cream
    - 1 egg
    - 1 tablespoon melted butter

- **Coconut Cream:**
    - 1 can (13.5 oz) full-fat coconut milk, refrigerated overnight
    - 1 tablespoon erythritol or your preferred sweetener (optional)
    - 1/2 teaspoon vanilla extract

- **Topping:**
  - 1 tablespoon erythritol or your preferred sweetener (optional)
  - 1/4 teaspoon vanilla extract
  - 1 cup fresh strawberries, sliced

Instructions:

1. **Prepare the shortcake:** Preheat your air fryer to 350°F (175°C). Combine the almond flour, coconut, erythritol, baking powder, and salt in a bowl.
2. In a separate bowl, whisk together the heavy cream, egg, and melted butter.
3. Pour the wet ingredients into the dry ingredients and mix until just combined. Do not overmix.
4. Divide the dough into four equal portions and shape each into a small disc or square.
5. Place the shortcake discs in the air fryer basket, ensuring they are not touching.
6. Air fry for 5 minutes, then flip and cook for another 5-7 minutes, or until golden brown and cooked throu
7. **While the shortcakes are cooking, prepare the coconut cream:** Scoop the thick, solidified coconut cre from the top of the refrigerated can. Leave the watery liquid at the bottom.
8. Beat the coconut cream with a whisk or electric mixer until light and fluffy. Add the sweetener (optional) vanilla extract.
9. **Assemble the shortcake:** Place a shortcake disc on each plate. Top with a generous dollop of coconut cr followed by sliced strawberries and a drizzle of sweetener and vanilla extract (optional).

Nutritional Information per serving: Calories: 450, Protein: 8g, Carbohydrates: 12g (5g net carbs), Fat: 35g, F 7g, Cholesterol: 60mg, Sodium: 200mg, Potassium: 250mg

9.10 Air Fryer Keto Banana Bread with Coconut Flour
Yield: 6 servings **Prep Time:** 10 minutes **Cook Time:** 20-25 minutes

Ingredients:

- 1/2 cup (1 stick) unsalted butter, softened
- 1/4 cup erythritol or your preferred keto-friendly sweetener
- 2 large eggs
- 1 teaspoon vanilla extract
- 1/2 teaspoon baking soda
- 1/4 teaspoon salt
- 1/2 cup unsweetened shredded coconut
- 1/4 cup almond flour
- 1/4 cup coconut flour
- 1/4 cup ground flaxseed meal
- 1/4 teaspoon cinnamon (optional, for added flavor)
- 1/4 cup chopped walnuts or pecans (optional, added texture)

Instructions:

1. Preheat your air fryer to 350°F (175°C).
2. In a large bowl, cream together the softened butter and erythritol until light and fluffy.
3. Beat in the eggs one at a time, then stir in the vanilla extract.
4. In a separate bowl, whisk together the baking soda, salt, coconut flour, almond flour, flaxseed meal, and cinnamon (if using).
5. Gradually add the dry ingredients to the wet ingredients, mixing until just combined. Be careful not to overmix.
6. Fold in the shredded coconut and chopped nuts (if using).

7. Spray your air fryer basket with non-stick cooking spray.
8. Transfer the batter to the air fryer basket and spread it evenly.
9. Cook for 15-20 minutes, shaking the basket halfway through to ensure even cooking.
10. To check for doneness, insert a toothpick into the center of the bread. If it comes out clean, it's ready.
11. Let the banana bread cool in the air fryer basket for a few minutes before transferring it to a wire rack to cool completely.

Nutritional Information per serving: Calories: 280, Protein: 6g, Carbohydrates: 10g (3g net carbs), Fat: 20g, Fiber: 3, Cholesterol: 50mg, Sodium: 100mg, Potassium: 150mg

10.10 Keto Chocolate Avocado Pudding
Yields: 2 servings **Prep Time:** 5 minutes **Cook Time:** 10 minutes

Ingredients:

- 1 ripe avocado, pitted and peeled
- 2 tbsp unsweetened cocoa powder
- 2 tbsp erythritol (or your preferred keto-friendly sweetener)
- 1/4 cup heavy whipping cream
- 1 tsp vanilla extract
- Pinch of salt
- Optional: 1/4 tsp cinnamon for added warmth

Instructions:

1. **Prep:** Combine all ingredients except the heavy whipping cream in a blender or food processor. Blend until smooth and creamy.
2. **Whip:** In a separate bowl, whip the heavy whipping cream until stiff peaks form.
3. **Fold:** Gently fold the whipped cream into the avocado mixture until evenly combined.
4. **Air Fry:** Pour the mixture into two small, heat-safe ramekins or bowls. Place the ramekins in the air fryer basket.
5. **Cook:** Air fry at 350°F (175°C) for 5-7 minutes, or until the pudding is set around the edges and slightly warmed through. You may need to adjust the cooking time based on your air fryer model.
6. **Chill:** Let the pudding cool slightly before transferring to the refrigerator to chill for at least 30 minutes for optimal texture and flavor.

Nutritional Information per Serving (Approximate): Calories: 300, Protein: 5 grams, Carbohydrates: 6 grams, Fats: 28 grams, Fiber: 4 grams, Cholesterol: 55 mg, Sodium: 50 mg, Potassium: 400 mg

11.10 Air Fryer Keto Apple Crisp with Almond Flour Topping
Yields: 4 servings **Prep Time:** 15 minutes **Cook Time:** 15-20 minutes

Ingredients:

- **Filling:**
    - 1/4 cup erythritol or stevia (to taste)
    - 1/4 teaspoon cinnamon
    - 1/8 teaspoon nutmeg
    - 1/4 teaspoon vanilla extract
    - 4 medium apples (such as Granny Smith or Honeycrisp), peeled, cored, and slice
    - 1 tablespoon lemon juice
- **Topping:**
    - 1/4 cup melted butter
    - 1/4 teaspoon cinnamon
    - 1/4 teaspoon salt
    - 1/2 cup almond flour
    - 1/4 cup unsweetened shredded coconut

Instructions:

1. **Prepare the filling:** In a large bowl, combine the sliced apples, lemon juice, erythritol or stevia, cinnamon, nutmeg, and vanilla extract. Mix well to coat the apples.
2. **Prepare the topping:** In a separate bowl, combine the almond flour, shredded coconut, melted butter, cinnamon, and salt. Mix well until evenly combined.
3. **Assemble the crisp:** Pour the apple mixture into an air fryer basket. Evenly distribute the topping mixture over the apples.
4. **Air fry:** Preheat your air fryer to 375°F (190°C). Air fry the apple crisp for 15-20 minutes, shaking the bas halfway through to ensure even cooking.
5. **Check for doneness:** The topping should be golden brown and the apples tender. If needed, air fry for an additional 2-3 minutes.
6. **Serve:** Let the apple crisp cool slightly before serving. Enjoy warm with a dollop of unsweetened whipped cream or a drizzle of sugar-free caramel sauce (optional).

Nutritional Information per serving (based on 4 servings): Calories: 350, Protein: 6 grams, Carbohydrates: 15 grams (3 grams net carbs), Fats: 25 grams, Fiber: 5 grams, Cholesterol: 30 mg, Sodium: 100 mg, Potassium: 200 r

12.10 Keto Coconut Flour Pancakes with Maple Syrup
Yield: 4 servings **Prep Time:** 5 minutes **Cook Time:** 5-7 minutes per pancake

Ingredients:

- 1/2 cup coconut flour
- 1/4 cup almond flour
- 1/4 cup erythritol or other keto-friendly sweetener
- 1 teaspoon baking powder
- 1/4 teaspoon salt
- 1 large egg
- 1/2 cup unsweetened almond milk
- 2 tablespoons melted coconut oil
- 1 teaspoon vanilla extract
- **Optional:** 1/4 teaspoon cinnamon (for warmth
- **Optional:** 1/4 cup chopped nuts (pecans, walnuts, etc.)

Keto Maple Syrup:
- 1/4 cup erythritol
- 1/4 cup water
- 1/4 teaspoon vanilla extract

1. **Prepare the Pancake Batter:** In a large bowl, whisk together the coconut flour, almond flour, erythritol, baking powder, and salt.
2. **Add Wet Ingredients:** In a separate bowl, whisk together the egg, almond milk, melted coconut oil, vanilla extract, and cinnamon (if using).
3. **Combine:** Gradually add the wet ingredients to the dry ingredients, mixing until just combined. Do not overmix.
4. **Stir in Nuts (optional):** If using, gently fold in the chopped nuts.
5. **Preheat Air Fryer:** Preheat your air fryer to 350°F (175°C). Lightly grease your air fryer basket with coconut oil or cooking spray.
6. **Cook Pancakes:** Pour 1/4 cup of batter into the air fryer basket for each pancake. Cook for 5-7 minutes per side, or until golden brown and cooked through. You may need to adjust the cooking time based on your air fryer.
7. **Make Maple Syrup:** While the pancakes cook, combine erythritol, water, and vanilla extract in a small saucepan. Bring to a simmer over medium heat, stirring constantly until the erythritol dissolves and the syrup thickens slightly.
8. **Serve:** Serve the pancakes hot with a generous drizzle of keto maple syrup.

Nutritional Information per Serving (without syrup): Calories: 250, Protein: 6 grams, Carbohydrates: 9 grams (3 grams net carbs), Fat: 18 grams, Fiber: 4 grams, Cholesterol: 40 mg, Sodium: 100 mg, Potassium: 200 mg

13.10 Air Fryer Keto Coconut Macaroons with Chocolate Drizzle
Yield: 12 macaroons **Prep Time:** 10 minutes **Cook Time:** 10-12 minutes

Ingredients:

- 1 cup unsweetened shredded coconut
- 1/4 cup almond flour
- 1/4 cup erythritol or other keto-friendly sweetener
- 1/4 cup melted coconut oil
- 1/4 teaspoon vanilla extract
- 1/4 teaspoon salt
- 1/4 cup sugar-free chocolate chips, melted (optional for drizzle)

Instructions:

1. **Prepare the batter:** In a large bowl, combine the shredded coconut, almond flour, erythritol, melted coconut oil, vanilla extract, and salt. Mix well until everything is evenly distributed.
2. **Form the macaroons:** Use a tablespoon to scoop out portions of the coconut mixture and roll them into balls. Arrange them in a single layer in the air fryer basket.
3. **Air fry:** Preheat your air fryer to 350°F (175°C). Place the macaroon balls in the air fryer basket and cook for 8-10 minutes, or until golden brown and slightly firm.
4. **Shake the basket:** Midway through cooking, gently shake the air fryer basket to ensure even browning.
5. **Chocolate drizzle (optional):** Once the macaroons are cooked, allow them to cool slightly. Melt the sugar-free chocolate chips and drizzle over the cooled macaroons for a decadent touch.
6. **Serve and enjoy:** Let the macaroons cool completely before serving.

Nutritional Information (per serving): Calories: 160, Protein: 1g, Carbohydrates: 5g (of which 2g is fiber), Fat: g, Cholesterol: 10mg, Sodium: 60mg, Potassium: 100mg

IV. Bonus Content

• Recipe Index

Keto Lentil Soup with Coconut Milk,76
Creamy Keto Chicken and Broccoli Soup,76
Keto Zuppa Toscana with Italian Sausage,78
Spicy Keto Buffalo Cauliflower Wings,29

CHEESE
Perfect Keto Omelet in a Flash,12
Easy Keto Egg Bites for Meal Prep,13
Cheesy Keto Breakfast Burrito,13
Keto Air Fryer Pizza Bites,17
Creamy Keto Chicken Parmesan,19
Creamy Keto Chicken Alfredo with Zucchini Noodles,22
Crispy Keto Zucchini Fries,25
Cheesy Keto Cauliflower Bites,25
Keto Air Fryer Onion Rings,26
Keto Avocado Fries,26
Air Fryer Keto Sweet Potato Fries,27
Crispy Keto Green Bean Fries,27
Chicken Caesar Salad with Creamy Parmesan Dressing,32
Air Fryer Roasted Vegetable Salad,34
Mediterranean Salad with Lemon Herb Vinaigrette,35
Air Fryer Roasted Butternut Squash Salad,37
Keto Spinach Salad with Strawberry Vinaigrette,37
Mediterranean Quinoa Salad with Feta and Kalamata Olives,38
Roasted Asparagus & Goat Cheese Salad with Honey-Mustard Dressing,40
Easy Keto Chicken Tenders,41
Air Fryer Turkey Taco Bowls with Cauliflower Rice,43
Air Fryer Turkey Pot Pie with Creamy Mushroom Sauce,45
Garlic Parmesan Keto Chicken Cutlets,46
Keto Chicken Parmesan with Low-Carb Breadcrumbs,47
Air Fryer Turkey Meatballs with Spicy Marinara Sauce,48
Crispy Keto Ground Beef Tacos,52
Easy Keto Meatballs with Marinara Sauce,53
Cheesy Keto Beef & Spinach Dip,55
Air Fryer Keto Beef Empanadas,56
Crispy Keto Air Fryer Fish & Chips,59
Air Fryer Keto Fish Sticks,60
Spicy Keto Tuna Cakes,61
Keto Steak Salad with Blue Cheese Dressing,65
Air Fryer Roasted Salmon Salad,66
Crispy Keto Air Fryer Tofu Scramble,68
Air Fryer Keto Vegetable Fritters,69
Keto Cauliflower Rice Pilaf,70
Crispy Air Fryer Tofu Nuggets with Sweet Chili

Sauce,70
Creamy Keto Spinach & Artichoke Dip,71
Garlic Parmesan Keto Broccoli Bites,72
Air Fryer Keto "Pasta" with Alfredo Sauce,73
Keto Avocado Toast with Smoked Paprika,74
Creamy Keto Chicken and Broccoli Soup,76
Spicy Keto Taco Soup,77
Keto Zuppa Toscana with Italian Sausage,78
Keto Creamy Mushroom Soup,80
Air Fryer Keto Pumpkin Soup,81
Keto Spinach and Artichoke Soup,82
Keto Shepherd's Pie with Cauliflower Mash,20
Air Fryer Keto Burgers with Low-Carb Buns,20
Keto Air Fryer Stuffed Peppers,21
Keto Cheese Curds,28
Spicy Keto Buffalo Cauliflower Wings,29
Cucumber & Dill Salad with Lemon-Herb Vinaigrette,38
Tomato & Basil Salad with Olive Oil & Balsamic Glaze,39
Easy Keto Fish Tacos with Avocado Crema,59
Air Fryer Keto Fish Burgers,63
Crispy Keto Zucchini Noodles with Pesto,72

CHERRIES
Easy Air Fryer Duck Breast with Cherry Sauce,46

CHERRY
Keto Fish & Veggie Skewers,61

CHIA SEEDS
Keto Smoothie Bowl with Berries & Nuts,14
Air Fryer Keto Chia Seed Pudding,14

CHICKEN BREAST
Creamy Keto Chicken and Broccoli Soup,76
Keto Chicken Salad with Avocado Dressing,24
Air Fryer Keto Chicken Fajitas,43
Air Fryer Keto Chicken Tikka Masala,47
Creamy Keto Chicken Alfredo with Zucchini Noodles,49
Keto Chicken Curry with Coconut Milk,51
Chicken Caesar Salad with Creamy Parmesan Dressing,32
Easy Keto Chicken Tenders,41
Garlic Parmesan Keto Chicken Cutlets,46
Air Fryer Keto Chicken Noodle Soup,82
Juicy Keto Air Fryer Chicken Breast,16
Creamy Keto Chicken Parmesan,19

reamy Keto Chicken Alfredo with Zucchini Noodles,22
emon Herb Keto Chicken Breast,42
eto Chicken Parmesan with Low-Carb Breadcrumbs,47

HICKEN BROTH
eto Beef & Broccoli Stir-Fry,23
ir Fryer Turkey Pot Pie with Creamy Mushroom Sauce,45
eto Fish Curry with Coconut Milk,62
reamy Keto Chicken and Broccoli Soup,76
eto Zuppa Toscana with Italian Sausage,78

HICKEN DRUMSTICKS
icy Keto Chicken Drumsticks,44

HIVES
una & Avocado Salad with Spicy Mayo & Sliced Eggs,36
cumber & Dill Salad with Lemon-Herb Vinaigrette,38
hicken Caesar Salad with Creamy Parmesan Dressing,32
eto Avocado Toast with Smoked Paprika,74

HOCOLATE CHIPS
eto Air Fryer Chocolate Chip Cookies,85
r Fryer Keto Coconut Macaroons with Chocolate Drizzle,9

LANTRO
r Fryer Keto Chicken Fajitas,43
r Fryer Keto Steak Fajitas,58
icy Keto Fish Tacos with Mango Salsa,63
uffy Keto Pancakes in Minutes,10
vory Keto Breakfast Hash,10
reamy Keto Avocado Toast,11
to Chicken Curry with Coconut Milk,51
sy Keto Fish Tacos with Avocado Crema,59
sy Keto Fish Tacos with Avocado Crema,59
to Fish Curry with Coconut Milk,62
ispy Keto Air Fryer Tofu Scramble,68
sy Keto Vegetable Curry,68
icy Air Fryer Tofu Scramble with Peppers and Onions,73
to Lentil Soup with Coconut Milk,76
cy Keto Taco Soup,77
cy Keto Chili with Ground Beef,83

NNAMON
Fryer Keto Cinnamon Rolls,11
Fryer Keto Chia Seed Pudding,14
spy Keto French Toast Sticks,15
Fryer Keto Pumpkin Soup,81
Fryer Keto Apple Crisp with Almond Flour Topping,92
Fryer Keto Sweet Potato Fries,27
Fryer Keto Macadamia Nut Brittle,30

Air Fryer Keto Banana Bread with Coconut Flour,90
Keto Chocolate Avocado Pudding,91
Keto Coconut Flour Pancakes with Maple Syrup,92

COCONUT
Air Fryer Keto Macadamia Nut Brittle,30

COCONUT FLOUR
Air Fryer Keto Cinnamon Rolls,11
Keto Air Fryer Chocolate Chip Cookies,85
Keto Pumpkin Spice Muffins,89
Air Fryer Keto Banana Bread with Coconut Flour,90
Keto Coconut Flour Pancakes with Maple Syrup,92

COCONUT MILK
Keto Smoothie Bowl with Berries & Nuts,14
Keto Chicken Curry with Coconut Milk,51
Keto Fish Curry with Coconut Milk,62
Easy Keto Vegetable Curry,68
Keto Lentil Soup with Coconut Milk,76
Keto Pumpkin Spice Muffins,89
Keto Strawberry Shortcake with Coconut Cream,89

COCONUT OIL
Fluffy Keto Pancakes in Minutes,10
Keto Smoothie Bowl with Berries & Nuts,14
Air Fryer Keto Chia Seed Pudding,14
Keto Avocado Fries,26
Keto Lemon Bars with Almond Flour Crust,87
Keto Pumpkin Spice Muffins,89
Keto Coconut Flour Pancakes with Maple Syrup,92
Air Fryer Keto Coconut Macaroons with Chocolate Drizzle,93

COD FILLETS
Air Fryer Keto Fish Sticks,60
Crispy Keto Air Fryer Fish & Chips,59
Easy Keto Fish Tacos with Avocado Crema,59
Keto Fish Curry with Coconut Milk,62
Spicy Keto Fish Tacos with Mango Salsa,63

CREAM CHEESE
Air Fryer Keto Cinnamon Rolls,11
Creamy Keto Chicken Alfredo with Zucchini Noodles,49
Creamy Keto Spinach & Artichoke Dip,71
Air Fryer Keto Stuffed Bell Peppers,74
Keto Raspberry Cheesecake Bites,85

CROUTONS
Chicken Caesar Salad with Creamy Parmesan Dressing,32

Keto Spinach Salad with Strawberry Vinaigrette,37
Mediterranean Quinoa Salad with Feta and
Kalamata Olives,38
Roasted Asparagus & Goat Cheese Salad with
Honey-Mustard Dressing,40
Crispy Air Fryer Duck Confit with Orange Glaze,42
Lemon Herb Keto Chicken Breast,42
Air Fryer Turkey Taco Bowls with Cauliflower Rice,43
Air Fryer Keto Chicken Fajitas,43
Spicy Keto Chicken Drumsticks,44
Air Fryer Turkey Pot Pie with Creamy Mushroom Sauce,45
Garlic Parmesan Keto Chicken Cutlets,46
Easy Air Fryer Duck Breast with Cherry Sauce,46
Air Fryer Keto Chicken Tikka Masala,47
Creamy Keto Chicken Alfredo with Zucchini Noodles,49
Keto Chicken Curry with Coconut Milk,51
Juicy Keto Air Fryer Steak with Garlic Herb Butter,52
Crispy Keto Ground Beef Tacos,52
Spicy Keto Chili with Ground Beef,53
Air Fryer Keto Beef & Broccoli Stir-Fry,54
Flavorful Keto Beef Brisket,55
Cheesy Keto Beef & Spinach Dip,55
Air Fryer Keto Beef Empanadas,56
Air Fryer Keto Steak Fajitas,58
Crispy Keto Air Fryer Fish & Chips,59
Easy Keto Fish Tacos with Avocado Crema,59
Keto Fish & Veggie Skewers,61
Keto Fish Curry with Coconut Milk,62
Spicy Keto Fish Tacos with Mango Salsa,63
Keto Fish & Chips with Cauliflower Mash,64
Keto Salmon with Roasted Vegetables,65
Keto Steak Salad with Blue Cheese Dressing,65
Air Fryer Roasted Salmon Salad,66
Crispy Air Fryer Mackerel with Lemon and Dill,67
Sardines: Air Fryer Sardines with Garlic and Herbs,67
Crispy Keto Air Fryer Tofu Scramble,68
Easy Keto Vegetable Curry,68
Keto Cauliflower Rice Pilaf,70
Crispy Keto Zucchini Noodles with Pesto,72
Garlic Parmesan Keto Broccoli Bites,72
Spicy Air Fryer Tofu Scramble with Peppers and Onions,73
Air Fryer Keto Stuffed Bell Peppers,74
Keto Lentil Soup with Coconut Milk,76
Creamy Keto Chicken and Broccoli Soup,76

Spicy Keto Taco Soup,77
Keto Zuppa Toscana with Italian Sausage,78
Keto French Onion Soup with Air Fryer Croutons,79
Keto Creamy Mushroom Soup,80
Air Fryer Keto Pumpkin Soup,81
Air Fryer Keto Chicken Noodle Soup,82
Keto Spinach and Artichoke Soup,82
Spicy Keto Chili with Ground Beef,83
Perfect Keto Omelet in a Flash,12
Easy Keto Meatballs with Marinara Sauce,53
Spicy Keto Tuna Cakes,61
Air Fryer Keto Vegetable Fritters,69

OLIVES
Mediterranean Salad with Lemon Herb Vinaigrette,
Mediterranean Quinoa Salad with Feta and
 Kalamata Olives,38
Tomato & Basil Salad with Olive Oil & Balsamic
 Glaze,39

ONION
Savory Keto Breakfast Hash,10
Sweet & Spicy Keto Breakfast Sausage,12
Easy Keto Ground Beef Stir-Fry,17
Keto Shepherd's Pie with Cauliflower Mash,20
Air Fryer Keto Burgers with Low-Carb Buns,20
Keto Air Fryer Stuffed Peppers,21
Keto Chicken Salad with Avocado Dressing,24
Keto Air Fryer Onion Rings,26
Mediterranean Salad with Lemon Herb Vinaigrette
Tuna & Avocado Salad with Spicy Mayo & Sliced
Eggs,36
Mediterranean Quinoa Salad with Feta and
Kalamata Olives,38
Cucumber & Dill Salad with Lemon-Herb
Vinaigrette,38
Tomato & Basil Salad with Olive Oil & Balsamic
Glaze,39
Air Fryer Keto Chicken Fajitas,43
Air Fryer Turkey Pot Pie with Creamy Mushroom
 Sauce,45
Air Fryer Turkey Meatballs with Spicy Marinara
Sauce,48
Keto Turkey Chili with Black Beans & Avocado,5
Keto Chicken Curry with Coconut Milk,51
Easy Keto Meatballs with Marinara Sauce,53
Spicy Keto Chili with Ground Beef,53
Cheesy Keto Beef & Spinach Dip,55

Easy Keto Fish Tacos with Avocado Crema,59
Keto Steak Salad with Blue Cheese Dressing,65
Creamy Keto Avocado Toast,11
Air Fryer Turkey Taco Bowls with Cauliflower Rice,43
Keto Turkey Chili with Black Beans & Avocado,50

SPINACH
Keto Spinach Salad with Strawberry Vinaigrette,37
Cheesy Keto Beef & Spinach Dip,55
Creamy Keto Spinach & Artichoke Dip,71
Air Fryer Keto Stuffed Bell Peppers,74
Keto Spinach and Artichoke Soup,82
Perfect Keto Omelet in a Flash,12
Keto Zuppa Toscana with Italian Sausage,78

STEAK
Keto Beef & Broccoli Stir-Fry,23
Juicy Keto Air Fryer Steak with Garlic Herb Butter,52
Air Fryer Keto Beef & Broccoli Stir-Fry,54
Air Fryer Keto Steak Fajitas,58
Keto Steak Salad with Blue Cheese Dressing,65

STRAWBERRIES
Keto Spinach Salad with Strawberry Vinaigrette,37
Keto Strawberry Shortcake with Coconut Cream,89

SWEET POTATO
Air Fryer Keto Sweet Potato Fries,27

T

TILAPIA
Keto Fish & Veggie Skewers,61
Air Fryer Keto Fish Burgers,63

TOFU
Crispy Keto Air Fryer Tofu Scramble,68
Crispy Air Fryer Tofu Nuggets with Sweet Chili Sauce,70
Spicy Air Fryer Tofu Scramble with Peppers and Onions,73

TOMATO
Air Fryer Keto Burgers with Low-Carb Buns,20
Easy Keto Fish Tacos with Avocado Crema,59
Caprese Salad with Balsamic Glaze,33
Mediterranean Salad with Lemon Herb Vinaigrette,35
Easy Keto Kale Salad with Parmesan,35
Tomato & Basil Salad with Olive Oil & Balsamic Glaze,39
Air Fryer Turkey Taco Bowls with Cauliflower

Rice,43
Air Fryer Keto Chicken Tikka Masala,47
Air Fryer Turkey Meatballs with Spicy Marinara Sauce,48
Keto Turkey Chili with Black Beans & Avocado,50
Spicy Keto Chili with Ground Beef,53
Air Fryer Keto Beef Empanadas,56
Air Fryer Roasted Salmon Salad,66
Spicy Keto Taco Soup,77
Spicy Keto Chili with Ground Beef,83

TORTILLAS
Spicy Keto Taco Soup,77

TUNA
Spicy Keto Tuna Cakes,61
Tuna & Avocado Salad with Spicy Mayo & Sliced Eggs,36

W

WALNUTS
Air Fryer Roasted Butternut Squash Salad,37
Keto Spinach Salad with Strawberry Vinaigrette,37
Keto Smoothie Bowl with Berries & Nuts,14
Air Fryer Keto Chia Seed Pudding,14
Keto Chicken Salad with Avocado Dressing,24
Air Fryer Roasted Vegetable Salad,34
Easy Keto Kale Salad with Parmesan,35
Roasted Asparagus & Goat Cheese Salad with Honey-Mustard Dressing,40
Keto Steak Salad with Blue Cheese Dressing,65
Air Fryer Keto Banana Bread with Coconut Flour,9

Z

ZUCCHINI
Creamy Keto Chicken Alfredo with Zucchini Noodles,22
Crispy Keto Zucchini Fries,25
Air Fryer Roasted Vegetable Salad,34
Creamy Keto Chicken Alfredo with Zucchini Noodles,49
Keto Salmon with Roasted Vegetables,65
Easy Keto Vegetable Curry,68
Crispy Keto Zucchini Noodles with Pesto,72
Air Fryer Keto Vegetable Fritters,69

• Air Fryer Tops&Cooking Temp Guide

ppetizers & Snacks:

Air Fryer Chicken Wings: 400°F (200°C) for 12-15 minutes, flipping halfway through.

Crispy Onion Rings: 400°F (200°C) for 6-8 minutes, flipping halfway through.

Air Fryer Mozzarella Sticks: 375°F (190°C) for 5-7 minutes, until golden brown and melted inside.

Air Fryer French Fries: 400°F (200°C) for 10-12 minutes, shaking halfway through.

Air Fryer Tater Tots: 400°F (200°C) for 8-10 minutes, shaking halfway through.

Air Fryer Sweet Potato Fries: 400°F (200°C) for 10-12 minutes, shaking halfway through.

ain Courses:

Air Fryer Chicken Breast: 375°F (190°C) for 12-15 minutes, flipping halfway through.

Air Fryer Salmon: 400°F (200°C) for 8-10 minutes, depending on thickness.

Air Fryer Steak: 400°F (200°C) for 5-8 minutes per side, depending on thickness and desired doneness.

Air Fryer Pork Chops: 375°F (190°C) for 10-12 minutes, flipping halfway through.

egetables:

Air Fryer Brussels Sprouts: 400°F (200°C) for 15-20 minutes, shaking halfway through.

Air Fryer Asparagus: 400°F (200°C) for 8-10 minutes, until tender and slightly browned.

Air Fryer Broccoli: 400°F (200°C) for 8-10 minutes, shaking halfway through.

Air Fryer Cauliflower: 400°F (200°C) for 10-12 minutes, shaking halfway through.

sserts:

Air Fryer Apple Fritters: 350°F (175°C) for 5-7 minutes, until golden brown.

Air Fryer Banana Bread: 350°F (175°C) for 15-20 minutes, until a toothpick inserted comes out clean.

Air Fryer Churros: 375°F (190°C) for 5-7 minutes, until golden brown and crispy.

Air Fryer Doughnuts: 350°F (175°C) for 4-6 minutes, until golden brown and puffed.

os:

- Use parchment paper in the basket to prevent sticking and make cleanup easier.
- Season your food generously for maximum flavor.
- Adjust cooking times as needed based on the size and type of food you are preparing.
- Watch your food closely during cooking to prevent burning.
- Don't overcrowd the basket, as this can affect air circulation and lead to uneven cooking.

• Top 9 Favorite Keto-friendly Nuts

Calorie and macronutrient breakdown for 100 grams of each nut:

Nut	Calories	Fat (grams)	Protein (grams)	Carbs (grams)
Macadamia Nuts	728	77.2	7.1	14.0
Pecans	691	72.0	10.4	13.6
Brazil Nuts	684	68.1	14.3	14.7
Pine Nuts	678	67.3	12.5	14.3
Walnuts	666	66.6	15.5	14.0
Hazelnuts	638	62.0	13.3	22.6
Almonds	584	51.1	21.5	21.5
Pistachios	560	45.5	20.5	28.7
Cashews	564	44.6	15.5	30.9

Made in the USA
Las Vegas, NV
12 January 2025

16267374R00059